M000308728

ADVANCE PRAISE

"CSU-Global is a pioneer in competency-based education. The university, under Dr. Takeda-Tinker's leadership, acknowledged a need within the growing nontraditional student population and created a model of education to serve them. Because of CSU-Global, thousands of professionals have been able to reinvent themselves for the twenty-first-century workforce. The university provides a cost-effective, time-efficient option to attain a degree, and schools across the nation could learn from its successes."

—JARED POLIS, US REPRESENTATIVE OF COLORADO

"Working with Becky and CSU-Global has been like collaborating with a world-class start-up. CSU-Global is a unique university that drives innovation with its stakeholders, partners, and the industry. The work of the institution over the last few years has been incredible, and I am pleased to see that the leadership is now sharing its insights and discoveries toward newer and workplace-relevant models of higher education."

—MARK PROTUS, DIRECTOR OF MODERN
LEARNING & VIDEO, MICROSOFT

IMPACTING THE FUTURE
OF HIGHER EDUCATION

IMPACTING
THE FUTURE OF
HIGHER
EDUCATION

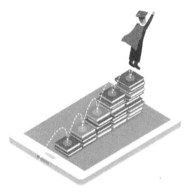

Insight Into a New Model That

Works *for* Students, Academic Institutions

and America

BECKY TAKEDA-TINKER

FOREWORD BY JON M. BELLUM, PHD

LIONCREST
PUBLISHING

COPYRIGHT © 2017 BECKY TAKEDA-TINKER

All rights reserved.

IMPACTING THE FUTURE OF HIGHER EDUCATION

Insight into a New Model that Works for Students,
Academic Institutions, and America

ISBN   978-1-61961-743-8 *Paperback*

978-1-61961-744-5 *Ebook*

This book is dedicated to the following individuals, without whom my work, and CSU-Global's success, would not have been possible:

The past and present students of CSU-Global, who have lived our ongoing evolution and who are thriving in our global marketplace. We take great pride in your individual and collective workplace success.

The Colorado State University System Board of Governors and the CSU Chancellors, past and present, for providing me with the latitude to lead and to envision what CSU-Global can and could be.

The CSU-Global staff and faculty, past and present. Through their daily work with the best interests of our students in mind, the university is the amazing institution that it is today.

Colorado community leaders and stakeholders who have provided unwavering support, even in our very early years: Senator Nancy Todd; Senator Chris Holbert; Congressman Jared Polis; Senator Michael Bennet; and our Advisory Council members, past and present.

Dr. Jon Bellum. His saying, "Just one more hurdle to clear," has led to my ongoing journey at CSU-Global, and his savvy in academia has provided immeasurable value in helping ensure the stability of the university against all odds.

My husband, Allen R. Tinker, who understands and respects my decision to lead the university as a contribution toward American competitiveness through the success of a new model of higher education.

My father, one of the early nontraditional students of our times; and my mother, who always thought I should be an educator.

CONTENTS

FOREWORD

BY JON M. BELLUM, PHD

When we're young, we feel that the days are long. But looking back, we realize that the years are short. In nearly a decade of my working alongside Becky Takeda-Tinker and a dynamic team to create CSU-Global from the ground up, there is nowhere else I would have wanted to be.

It sounds like something out of an old black-and-white movie, but, truly, when I was looking for a new job, it was as if a light shone on a job ad at what was then called CSU-Colorado. I was in traditional academia, and I knew immediately that I wanted to help create this one-of-a-kind public university for nontraditional students. I accepted the job, packed up my young family, moved from Vermont to Colorado, and began work—all in three weeks. That's how committed and excited I was to be a part of this venture.

Becky and I began at CSU-Global together, and together we left for a year when the political winds shifted. But I told those left behind that I would leave the lights on in my office, and I jumped at the chance to return. Happily, for me and for CSU-Global, Becky also came back.

I can honestly say that CSU-Global exists as the successful university it is today in large part because Becky was the right person at the right time. She had the background in business and private equity to turn us around—to take an institution with a great idea but shaky finances and put us on solid footing. She took a huge risk, righted the ship, and could easily have moved on.

But Becky didn't leave, because she, like our hardworking and dedicated staff and faculty, believes in the mission and vision of CSU-Global—that our one and only job is to *prepare nontraditional learners for workplace success in a global marketplace through education.* We exist to provide what our students need in the way that they need it. The fact that we are the first, and currently the only, fully accredited online public university that receives no state support is a testament to her leadership of the CSU-Global stakeholders and our collective, unwavering dedication to our students.

In the pages of this book, Becky lays out for other risk-takers what it means to reimagine higher education for adult learners. She doesn't mince words—this work isn't for the faint of heart. But she is very clear about the bottom line. When you serve your students, you ensure their success, and yours. I'm proud to have played my part in this story.

The journey has not been easy, but it has made me realize that the distance between a vision and reality is achievable with a lot of hard work by determined individuals. I hope that the CSU-Global story inspires and challenges those following the status quo to think and act differently in order to truly transform higher education, because success in our modern world requires it.

—JON M. BELLUM, PHD
PROVOST AND EXECUTIVE VICE PRESIDENT
COLORADO STATE UNIVERSITY–GLOBAL CAMPUS

PREFACE

A VISION

To this day, I'm not certain whether I chose education or education chose me. What I do know is that I wanted to inspire students to do something great, to add value to the workplace, and to help ensure ongoing American competitiveness.

At the same time, I knew that making a difference in the life of even a single student was a worthwhile objective. I thought I could make an important contribution, even if I did nothing more than help one student at a time succeed.

Working in the world of business and private equity, I've traveled the world. I've seen how important higher education is to citizens of other countries. Every time I returned home, however, I was struck by the fact that fewer American students were attending college[1] and that American business leaders, including myself, were dissatisfied with their newly minted graduates. So, rather than continue to complain about the state of higher education in America, I decided I should do something about it.

I did my research. I learned that a doctorate degree was the key to success in higher education, so I began that journey.

I planned to work at a community college. I wanted to engage and inspire students who didn't get into or didn't want to attend a four-year school. I hoped that I could help them graduate and perhaps continue on to get their bachelor's degree. That was my plan—until, one day, I got a call out of the blue.

THE BEGINNING

Someone must have heard about me or found me on LinkedIn, because within a couple of months after moving to Colorado, I received a call asking if I would do some work for a new online university that was going to serve

[1]   In this book, the term "college" is used broadly to refer to institutions for graduate and undergraduate education and is used interchangeably with the term "university." In the higher education industry, however, the term "college" typically refers to institutions that award associate degrees, while the term "university" refers to institutions that award four-year and graduate degrees. The term "postsecondary education" may refer to any post-high school institution, including colleges, universities, trade schools, and technical and career colleges.

adults. They needed a practitioner who had been in business and leadership positions to create curriculum in those content areas.

I was compelled to contribute to their effort because of my father. During World War II, my dad and his family were sent to internment camps. After the war ended, they were released but didn't have any assets, so they all worked in a hotel to help keep a roof over their heads. That lifestyle convinced my dad that he needed to go to college to better his life. While at the University of California, Berkeley, he worked to pay for his tuition and living expenses, thereby restricting his university participation.

I realized that my dad could have benefited from the anytime, anywhere, 100 percent online education offered by the Colorado State University–Global Campus (CSU-Global). At least with CSU-Global, he could have interacted with instructors and peers to have more of a real college experience, and he may not have had to work such long hours due to the low costs and flexibility of this type of online program. With that in mind, I agreed to get involved and, in May 2008, I showed up at CSU-Global to begin work on several courses.

I loved it. It was a fun, unique environment with an entrepreneurial spirit that was familiar to me. That September, the university opened to about two hundred students. I stayed until January 2009, when the political winds shifted, and I moved on to teach and help develop curricula at other institutions.

THE TURNAROUND

The CSU System Board of Governors initially funded CSU-Global in 2007 with a loan of $12 million. By state statute, the fifteen-member board includes nine voting members appointed by the Colorado governor. The Board of Governors presides over the three universities in the system, which, in addition to CSU-Global, includes a research institution, CSU in Fort Collins, and a regional institution, CSU-Pueblo.

In July 2009, I learned that CSU-Global was at risk of closing. The university had spent the loan monies provided by the Board of Governors, and it appeared that the board was not going to provide additional financial support. The country was in the midst of a recession, and several other online state educational institutions had closed. It looked as if CSU-Global would be another casualty.

Without an additional cash infusion, the campus required restructuring and a fresh perspective. With my strong belief in the university's mission and in what the institution could become, I rejoined CSU-Global. Together with the help of the faculty, staff, and Dr. Jon Bellum, who went on to become our provost, we reorganized and reallocated resources. We established a singular focus on our students, their satisfaction, and their academic success. These actions helped ensure that our students had a positive experience, would remain with us to complete their degrees, and would recommend the university to their family and friends. Our focus on our students' satisfaction and success has become firmly rooted in our culture, and 30 percent of our new students still come from referrals.

VALUES DRIVEN

Since I returned to CSU-Global, we have experienced rapid and dynamic growth. Our nontraditional students are savvy and outspoken. The pace of technological change is unrelenting. We have managed our evolution by adopting a set of six core values, developed by the forty or so faculty and staff we had at the beginning and endorsed by all who have joined us since. These values are the cornerstone of our culture and keep us solidly anchored as we continue to grow.

- We are focused squarely on our **mission**. CSU-Global exists to serve its students, and they are our highest priority.
- Our nontraditional students deserve **innovative thinking** that

combines the best of what higher education and industry have to offer.

- 🍎 To ensure our students' success, we hold one another **accountable** to our mission, our students, and the university.

- 🍎 **Collaboration** isn't just a catchphrase at CSU-Global—it is at the heart of how we work together, learn from one another, and respect each other's contributions.

- 🍎 We are never static; we are continually **learning** and **growing**, reflecting the value of lifelong learning that our students embrace.

- 🍎 **Professionalism** in all that we do guides our interactions with one another, with our students, and with our colleagues. We follow the "golden rule."

The focus on our mission, our ability to be accountable to and collaborate with one another, our drive to continually learn and grow, and our pledge to manage change in a professional manner—this is the glue that binds us at CSU-Global. Our core values allow us to be champions for our nontraditional students and to be catalysts for change in higher education.

EDUCATION THAT WORKS

My background in putting organizations on solid footing uniquely positioned me to help CSU-Global survive the difficult times and become the thriving organization it is today. Together, CSU-Global stakeholders and I fully embrace our shared mission of workplace success through higher education for nontraditional students. *I believe in that mission.* I believe we have to reach the nontraditional student: the student for whom going away to school and living in a dorm is an unaffordable luxury, or for whom higher education is believed to be an unattainable dream because they lack the necessary support infrastructure. The student who is working and helping to support a family, who lives overseas, or who has joined the armed forces to defend our country and protect the freedoms the rest of us enjoy, the student who has arrived in this country in search of a better life—these are the students CSU-Global serves.

We put education within these students' reach. We are online, not because we want to label CSU-Global an online university, nor to compete with for-profit online schools. We are online because our adult students need to be able to take classes anytime, from anywhere. We offer guaranteed tuition because our students need college to be affordable; notably, for our fiscal year 2018, we will enter our sixth year without a tuition increase. We provide a single point of contact to help our students successfully navigate university processes and policies, and we welcome students with diverse needs because our students need college to be accessible. We offer free career facilitation because *we are in business to help our students succeed.*

At CSU-Global, we know whom we serve, and we are driven to serve them in the best way possible. This is what makes CSU-Global unique, but it's also a prescription for success in all of higher education. Whether you are a student, a family member, an administrator in charge of an academic institution, or a concerned citizen, this book is for you. Together, we can launch new models of education so that it works—for our students and their families, for our businesses, and for our country. Our success as a nation depends on it.

INTRODUCTION

A NEW MODEL

———

There is a crisis in higher education, and it didn't happen overnight. For years, we have been seeing the impact of three major trends.

First, the number of adults with some college education but no degree continues to rise. Out of every one hundred students who start college, only slightly more than half earn a degree.[1] Today, there are more than 44 million Americans who attended college but never completed their degrees.[2] That's a huge problem. Each of these indi-

———

1   D. Shapiro et al., "Completing College: A National View of Student Attainment Rates—Fall 2009 Cohort," (Herndon, VA: National Student Clearinghouse Research Center, 2015), https://nscresearchcenter.org/signaturereport10/.

2   "Educational Attainment," United States Census Bureau, March 2017, https://www.census.gov/topics/education/educational-attainment.html.

viduals began school with a goal in mind: to finish their degree and get a job or advance in their career. But they didn't finish for one reason or another, usually because they ran out of time or money. So, now they have nothing to show for the time and money they have already invested.

The research on for-profit educational institutions is equally troubling.[3] It was this sector that first aggressively sought to serve nontraditional students with fully online options. However, a US Senate report published in 2012 concluded that fewer than 50 percent of students who enrolled in for-profit institutions were retained beyond four months. Even more concerning is the fact that while 96 percent of students who attended for-profit institutions used federal loans, 47 percent have already defaulted on their loans, and only one in four students who have not been identified as being in default has actually made a payment.

CSU-Global works with students seeking to transfer from for-profit institutions; and it is not surprising to find that these students are far from degree completion, but near the end of their federal loan limit, which currently stands at $57,500 for undergraduates and $138,500 for grad-

---

3   "Executive Summary," U.S. Senate, accessed July 9, 2017, https://www.help.senate.gov/imo/media/for_profit_report/ExecutiveSummary.pdf.

uates.[4] CSU-Global understands its responsibility as a nonprofit state institution to help these students, and it has created innovative pathways to do so.

All told, American students are carrying an estimated outstanding balance of $1.31 trillion in federal student loan debt,[5] and nearly $30 billion in Pell Grants were awarded in fiscal year 2016.[6] No matter where they have studied, it's important that students successfully complete their degrees or certificate programs in order to find the type of high-paying positions that will allow them to repay the taxpayers who have funded their educations.

Second, there has been a shift from the traditional student who attends school full time to the nontraditional or modern student who attends school while working and raising a family. Today, only about 25 percent of students attend school full time directly out of high school,[7] yet the majority of US higher education institutions are built for this ever-diminishing group.

---

4   "The U.S. Department of Education Offers Low-Interest Loans to Eligible Students to Help Cover the Cost of College or Career School," Federal Student Aid, accessed July 9, 2017, https://studentaid.ed.gov/sa/types/loans/subsidized-unsubsidized.

5   Zach Friedman, "Student Loan Debt in 2017: A $1.3 Trillion Crisis," Forbes, February 21, 2017, https://www.forbes.com/sites/zackfriedman/2017/02/21/student-loan-debt-statistics-2017/.

6   Bob Pfeiffer, "Pell Grants," Federal Safety Nets, accessed July 9, 2017, http://federalsafetynet.com/pell-grants.html.

7   U.S. Department of Education, "Definitions and Data," National Center for Education Statistics, accessed July 9, 2017, https://nces.ed.gov/pubs/web/97578e.asp.

The majority of traditional academic institutions were built on a factory model to serve post-World War II Americans. Students got on the conveyor belt at point A. As long as they stayed on the conveyor belt and did exactly what they were told, they graduated, and that conveyor belt put them right into a job at point B. But this is no longer the way the world works, nor the way the majority of students actually participate in higher education.

There is ever-increasing and global competition for jobs, and most jobs today require the ability and expertise to be "plug and play." College graduates without skills to readily step into jobs end up unemployed or underemployed. Higher education is no longer a golden ticket to fulfill their dreams. In fact, more than half—51 percent—of college graduates are working at jobs that do not require a degree, and only 27 percent are working in jobs related to their degree programs.[8]

At the other end of the spectrum are students increasingly unable to afford higher education, and those who become disillusioned because they have difficulty navigating the traditional college environment. They don't have time to go to three different offices, one to enroll, another to sign up for courses, and a third to pay. Without a college

---

8   "The State of American Jobs," Pew Research Center, October 6, 2016, http://www.pewsocialtrends.org/2016/10/06/the-state-of-american-jobs/.

degree, they end up in lower-sector service jobs. Many of these jobs are quickly going away or being outsourced to other countries that have significantly lower costs of living and, therefore, lower wages and business costs.

As a case in point, tollbooth collectors are largely obsolete. Hotels are using robots as concierges. Call centers have spread like wildfire in English-speaking countries around the world. Soon, we won't need people to make our fast-food hamburgers, because that, too, will be handled by robots. Most important, the pace of technological change will only get faster.

Third, the public perception of the value of a college education continues to decline. Data compiled by Gallup are startling:[9]

- Eighty percent of Americans agree or strongly agree that colleges and universities need to change to better meet the needs of today's students.
- Seventy-nine percent of Americans do not think that education beyond high school is affordable for everyone in this country who needs it.

---

9   "What America Needs to Know about Higher Education Redesign: The 2013 Lumina Study of the American Public's Opinion on Higher Education and U.S. Business Leaders Poll on Higher Education," Lumina Foundation, February 25, 2014, https://www.luminafoundation.org/files/resources/2013-gallup-lumina-foundation-report.pdf.

- Only 50 percent of university graduates believe that higher education is worth the cost.
- Only 6 percent of Americans with degrees strongly agree that college graduates in this country are well prepared for success in the workplace.

Taken together, these facts make clear that innovation in higher education is needed to address the unmet and individual needs of students who have not or are not succeeding with the traditional models most readily available to them. But it's not enough to abandon the postwar conveyor-belt model of education. We must replace it with new and innovative models that more fully engage students, provide them with skills for workplace success, and make education affordable.

THE BEST OF BOTH WORLDS

If the American public doesn't think that higher education is worth the expense, how long will they continue to support it? Already, we're beginning to see a shift, with states publicly announcing their intention not to provide the funds needed to offset the true cost of public higher education.

In addition, some states are setting up or considering apprenticeship programs modeled on European approaches. In these states, instead of all high school students being directed to attend college, young people are guided to gain practical job skills with supplemental pathways for college courses. This is not necessarily a bad idea; the more options people have to be productive in the workplace, the better. But data from the US Bureau of Labor Statistics (BLS) show that employees with a bachelor's degree earn an average of 42.5 percent more than those with an associate's degree, and 67 percent more than those with a high school diploma.[10] Today's adult learners recognize the value of continuing their education to earn a degree and to learn relevant workplace skills.

Moreover, today's employers need skilled and educated workers. The BLS estimates that by 2020, 65 percent of jobs will require postsecondary education.[11] Increasingly, these jobs will demand critical thinking and independent decision making.

While higher education teaches critical-thinking skills, they are no longer enough. Today's graduates need to be able to step into a job on day one and do whatever tasks they are assigned. As the United States and other countries begin replacing people with robots, someone

10 "Employment Projections," Bureau of Labor Statistics, April 20, 2017, https://www.bls.gov/emp/ep_chart_001.htm.

11 C. Brett Lockard and Michael Wolf, "Occupational Employment Projections to 2020," *Monthly Labor Review* (January 2012), https://www.bls.gov/opub/mlr/2012/01/art5full.pdf.

has to create and lead the companies that use the robots. More important, we need people who can figure out what to do when things go wrong. The value of human workers is in their ability to apply critical-thinking skills to real-world scenarios.

What if we could blend these approaches? What if we could take the best of traditional academic education and combine it with the actual requirements of the marketplace to ensure that our graduates not only understand the theory of leadership, but are also able to lead? What if we could teach our students the research skills and critical thinking that are required to make effective decisions in and out of the classroom and, at the same time, get them the industry certifications that enable them to be "plug and play" in our increasingly global marketplace?

We can, and we must look at higher education with these metrics in mind. At CSU-Global, the university develops and intentionally teaches its students critical-thinking skills, and it measures improvement in this area from the time they enroll to the time they graduate. The institution develops its own programs and hires its own faculty to prepare students for in-demand jobs. The university also surveys employers about the success of its graduates, and it surveys graduates about their success, as measured both by career satisfaction and by salary increases. The university then makes improvements as needed to ensure graduate and employer satisfaction. All of this provides CSU-Global students with a return on their investment of both time and money, which we know is important to them based on student feedback and retention data.

CSU-Global has proven that there are ways to measure the importance of higher education. And it can demonstrate that its graduates succeed in the workplace.

NOT YOUR PARENT'S EDUCATION

The fact is, we have no choice but to rethink our approach to higher education. In the future, not all of our colleges and universities will be able to keep their doors open if they continue to try to serve an ever-declining population of traditional students. Recent university closures[12] confirm that this is no longer the world of the Baby Boomers, in which young people automatically left for college after they finished high school.

That's what I did. My parents instilled in me at a very early age that I needed to do well in school to get into a good college. I needed to do well in college so that I could get

---

12   Lindsey McKenzie, "2 More University Mergers Are Announced in Georgia," *The Chronicle of Higher Education*, January 11, 2017, http://www.chronicle.com/blogs/ ticker/2-more-university-mergers-are-announced-in-georgia/116424

a good job and support myself in the lifestyle that was at least equivalent to my upbringing. This was the factory, one-size-fits-all model of education, which no longer works for the large percentage of nontraditional students in our dynamic economy.

Today's students are living in the world the Baby Boomers have created. Members of Generations X and Y grew up with iTunes and computers. They expect everything to be personalized and customizable. They don't have to buy the whole record album the way I did when I was growing up. They can buy one song. They can now rent the version of the song they want. They can pick the artist and the format. And they can get it instantly. They can even customize the design of their running shoes and order just their favorite M&M colors.

The world has dramatically shifted, but higher education hasn't kept up. Most traditional academic institutions are still operating on the factory model. Even if they had a sudden influx of students, they wouldn't have the money to build more buildings to get those students into seats.

We must rethink our approach to higher education to meet the needs of today's modern students and address the challenges of our technologically driven and global marketplace, *because this country is not sustainable with an uneducated workforce.* We can no longer continue to churn out students who are not prepared to effectively assume positions in organizations. We can no longer afford to leave behind young adults who want and need a higher education, but who don't have the time or the money to complete their educational goals.

My fear is that we will end up with the type of social strata you see in third-world countries—with those at the very top doing well and those at the very bottom continuing to fall further behind. Higher education has a critical role to play in closing this gap. We can make education affordable and accessible, and we can measure our results. We not only can do so, but *we must do so.*

A MODEL FOR SUCCESS

At CSU-Global, the recipe for success is deceptively simple. *The institution knows the students it is serving, and it works every day to serve them well.* The university continuously improves its efforts to help its students achieve academic and workplace success.

To do so, CSU-Global focuses on what it calls its four pillars of success: *choice, transparency, service,* and *achievement.* The nontraditional students CSU-Global serves need the choice to study on their own schedule, not the university's. They need transparency in pricing, so they understand on day one what their coursework or degree or certificate program will cost. They expect the same type of customized and individualized experience they've come to expect from their cell phone companies or favorite retailers. And CSU-Global expects them to achieve success in the classroom and in the workplace, so it does everything in its power to make that success possible.

The balance of this book will show you how CSU-Global does this. The lessons are transferrable to any institution of higher education that aims to help its students succeed.

Chapter 1, "It's All about the Students," highlights the changing demographics of today's college students and the specific students CSU-Global is designed to serve. The message is simple: We must identify our market and give them what they need to succeed. CSU-Global does this by focusing on choice, transparency, service, and achievement.

Chapter 2, "Defining Success," makes the point that success should be defined by each institution according to its students, its mission, and the data it collects. Success that is benchmarked only to one's peers is destined to fall short, because if other institutions are equally unsuccessful in meeting their goals, it becomes a race to mediocrity.

Chapter 3, "Return on Investment," makes clear that today's students are intentional about the decision to get a college degree. They want value for their hard-earned money, and CSU-Global is intentional about providing it.

Chapter 4, "Data Is Nearly Everything," details not only the wealth of data that is collected at CSU-Global, but why it's so important to base decisions on what we know works. The university makes decisions based on the quantitative and qualitative data that support the best interests of its students, rather than simply on what the institutional leadership has decided it should do.

Chapter 5, "Faculty and Administration," highlights the fact that students whose goal is workplace success receive multiple benefits by learning from those who have actually worked. Traditional academic preparation is fine if the job is research. Students who want to study information technology (IT) to work in an IT department, however, gain immeasurably by learning from someone who has IT credentials paired with experience in all the challenges IT professionals face in the workplace.

Chapter 6, "Money and Time Matter," is where the rubber meets the road. Time and money are the two biggest reasons why students don't complete their degrees, their certificates, or even the few courses they intend to take.

CSU-Global strives to make higher education affordable. The university budget is based on what students need to achieve their goals, and it caps tuition and offers pay-as-you-go pricing. Students know what it will cost them to complete their education and achieve their goals before they take a single CSU-Global class.

Chapter 7, "Efficient and Ready for Scale," shows both how CSU-Global keeps costs low by eliminating unnecessary expenses and how it maximizes each student's time for learning by minimizing the time it takes them to negotiate the university's systems and processes.

Chapter 8, "Learning for Real Life," proves that outcome-based education not only can be done, but must be done. CSU-Global students expect to be successful, so the university rigorously assesses their ability to perform academically and in the working world. If they are not able to do so, it is considered a shared failure.

The conclusion, "What Comes After," looks ahead to a time when all institutions of higher education have learned what CSU-Global has proven to be true. Rather than taking existing products and trying to find a market, we must identify our students and develop products and services to meet their needs. Simply put, *we must know whom we are serving and serve them well.* Most important, we must continually and relentlessly strive to improve. Restoring American competitiveness in a global economy depends on us getting this right.

IT STARTS WITH OUR STUDENTS

CSU-Global has a prescription for success. It begins, first and foremost, with knowing the students it serves. Chapter 1 highlights how what the institution knows about its students is reflected in its programs and policies, and how this knowledge drives CSU-Global's ongoing innovation to facilitate student academic and workplace success.

1

IT'S ALL ABOUT THE STUDENTS

—

The process of earning a college degree could be like the experience of working with your financial advisor or tax accountant.

When you meet with your accountant, you have certain expectations. The first is that the accountant will provide you with insight and expertise, so that you will have choices in how the two of you will work together to calculate and file your taxes.

The second expectation is transparency. Your accountant will review your information and provide you with the cost for completing your tax forms. Based on intermittent touch points between the accountant and you, there are rarely any surprises when the invoice arrives.

The third expectation is service. You expect that your accountant will be prompt with the delivery of your information as previously agreed. He or she will be attentive and helpful.

Finally, you expect to achieve your objectives. You don't hire an accountant to have incomplete or inaccurate guidance. If you do get poor support, you'll take your business elsewhere. If enough people do this, the accountant will go out of business.

Choice, transparency, service, and *achievement.* These are the drivers of an education at CSU-Global. And, as with any good accountant, the institution meets its students' expectations because *it knows whom it is serving.* The university is not offering a four-year, sit-in-your-seat, live-in-the-dorm education to a student who is working, supporting a family, and trying to advance their career. That would be like providing life insurance advice to someone who just wants their taxes calculated and filed on time.

CHANGING STUDENTS, CHANGING TIMES

Gone are the days when the majority of students attend

a four-year college straight out of high school. Today, 75 percent of students are what we used to call "nontraditional," or contemporary, post-traditional students.

Most people would probably love to be able to live in a dorm and attend school full time. What an idyllic environment! Students are out of their parents' house. They have nearly unbridled freedom. They join clubs, they run associations, and maybe they have part-time jobs, all while they address their school responsibilities. This experience provides a four-to-five-year transition period for young adults to mature and grow, and to safely stretch their independence.

The nontraditional students CSU-Global serves, however, have priorities other than living on campus and going to school full time. They range in age from late teens to sixty-five, with an average age of thirty-four. Many have children at home. Often, they are caring for older family members, as well. They are diverse; they live in every US state and territory and fifty-four different countries.

Nationally, 30 percent of all students are the first in their families to attend college.[1] At CSU-Global, that number is up at 40 percent. Often, these students are trying to

---

1   Ioanna Opidee, "Supporting First-Gen College Students," *University Business*, February 25, 2015, https://www.universitybusiness.com/article/supporting-first-gen-college-students.

finish a degree that they started but didn't complete because they ran out of time or money, or they needed to attend to family matters that derailed their earlier college attendance.

Growing numbers of today's nontraditional college students are veterans or military-affiliated, including 15 percent of CSU-Global's student population. These students served their country and held specific jobs in the military, but they need to translate their experience to civilian service and upskill to meet private industry demands. They are also older than first-time college students.

Finally, these nontraditional or modern students include lifelong learners. They understand the importance of continually updating their skills in an ever-competitive, technologically driven workforce.

Technology has sped the rate of change around the world. When I first got into higher education, I learned that, generally, degree content needed to be updated every five years to stay relevant. However, CSU-Global faculty and its industry experts have determined degree content must be updated every twelve to twenty-four months to stay current in today's world.

Think about how different the world was just five years

ago, before the launch of Blue Apron and dinner supplies arriving at your doorstep, or Udacity and the concept of free and massively distributed learning. And think about how different it will be five years from now. Clearly, the value of a degree is continuing to shrink in time. Lifelong learning will no longer be something people do for fun—it will be what they must do for continued employment success.

CHOICE, TRANSPARENCY, SERVICE, AND ACHIEVEMENT: THE PILLARS OF SUCCESS

All of these students—those who are working and caring for their families, those who are relatively new to this country, those who have served their country, and those who are lifelong learners—share a common goal. They need on-demand access to a high-quality education that is affordable and designed to ensure their success, not only directly after graduation but throughout their careers. These are the students CSU-Global serves, and it does so by offering them the same type of service experiences they have come to expect from their other expert advisors.

CHOICE

At CSU-Global, students have a list of program options from which to choose, and they pick only what they want and need. If they want to take only one or two classes, they only pay for one or two classes. The university's approach is as simple as that.

Contrast that to traditional higher education, in which students pay a set amount for a full semester, regardless of how many classes they intend to take, or how many classes they are able to take with a high degree of success. In CSU-Global's view, this approach is like charging people for insurance advice and services, when they only wanted to get their past year's taxes calculated and filed.

Nontraditional students need flexibility. That's part of the reason CSU-Global starts a new eight-week term every month. Some students begin in January, aiming to complete their courses in March; others start in February, planning to finish in April. This is a huge undertaking. The university takes in hundreds of new students every month, while maintaining a focus on all its existing students, staying in contact with them, and getting them ready for the next term.

CSU-Global's doors are always open, because its students may need to take a break and then get right back into classes. Perhaps one of their family members gets sick, or their work schedule changes.

For nontraditional adult learners in most online environments, if they disengage for four months or more, it's very difficult for them to return. They have busy schedules, they fill those spaces of time quickly, and they may not come back to school. CSU-Global, however, has a year-round, compressed, eight-week schedule and an "every class every term" philosophy. This allows students to access classes when they feel they can successfully complete them, rather than when it might be convenient for staff and faculty to offer them.

Interestingly, the university's data show that when students disengage, they typically don't continue their education elsewhere. The university believes that's even worse than having them go to another institution and not return to CSU-Global. CSU-Global knows that students come to the university fully intending to complete their academic goals, so it makes navigating the school environment as smooth as possible, allowing students to focus on their classwork. The university's student retention rates prove that this works. Retention rates average 82 percent from the first trimester to the third trimester (from fall 2016 to winter 2016 to spring 2017).

TRANSPARENCY

There are some accountants who want to charge an hourly rate that will be totaled once they complete your taxes. That makes you a bit nervous about proceeding, doesn't it?

Now, consider traditional higher education, where average tuition continues to outpace the rate of inflation.[2] Student fees increase, and new ones are added. Students don't know from year to year what college will cost, and there may come a time in their college career when they simply can't afford it. The fact that 40 percent of higher education students do not complete their degrees, and that money is one of the two key reasons they disengage, indicates that cost does matter.

At CSU-Global, students know that "what they see is what they get." Personnel in the university's tuition planning department meet with each student when they enroll to figure out what their education will cost. For each incoming student, staff combine the information on how many credit hours the institution will accept for transfer, how many credits are needed to complete the student's identified degree, and how much those remaining credits will cost. Then, staff talk with each student about the various options both to reduce the cost of the degree and to cover the cost. CSU-Global tuition is also guaranteed—individual students never experience a tuition increase as long as

2   Jennifer Ma et al., "Trends in College Pricing 2016," College Board, 2016, accessed July 9, 2017, https://trends.collegeboard.org/sites/default/files/2016-trends-college-pricing-web_1.pdf.

they are continuously enrolled. As previously noted, 2018 will be the university's sixth consecutive year without a tuition increase.

Further, the university has no student fees. It doesn't charge for student activities, career coaching, or the graduation ceremony. Students do pay for their textbooks, but CSU-Global doesn't have a bookstore that's a profit center, so it does everything it can to make class resources as economical as possible. It gives its students information about renting books and purchasing used books, as well as about using e-chapters and e-books. It helps students find the least expensive, most practical way for them to get the resources they need.

CSU-Global's goal is simple. It never wants a student to have unexpected expenses that would cause them to say, "Well, I'm not going to reenroll, because I don't have that extra $500 this semester." The university wants its students to graduate or complete whatever academic goals they have and be successful in the workplace, so it works within their budgets to help them do so.

SERVICE

Think about your tax accountant or other professional expert advisor. Why do you keep using their services?

When you are pleased with the service you receive, you establish an ongoing and trusted working relationship. However, if the service is poor or inaccurate, you will find a different way to get the help you need.

CSU-Global is very clear that it exists for one reason, and one reason only—to serve its students. The university's primary objective, reflected in its mission, is *to prepare nontraditional learners for workplace success in a global marketplace through education.* It does that by offering the highest-quality education paired with unsurpassed, world-class service.

This begins when a student comes to the university's door. From the enrollment counselor to the tuition planning specialists, financial aid staff, student advisors, and class instructors, students have dedicated staff to help them enroll, budget, take courses, get extra help, and graduate or complete their academic goals.

CSU-Global students don't have to go one place to pay, another place to choose courses, and a third place for academic advising. Staff in these departments work behind the scenes with one another to make sure all students have what they need to succeed in class and at the university. Faculty have imposed their own accountability to students and require twenty-four-hour responses to student contact, seventy-two-hour turnaround on graded assignments, and classroom check-ins five out of seven days a week. CSU-Global students also have access to free career coaching and twenty-four-hour, seven-day-a-week live tutoring, technical support, and access to library staff.

For more traditional students, navigating the school's policies and processes becomes a job of its own. But CSU-Global students are working and caring for their families. Lack of time is one of the two key reasons students disengage, and these students don't have time to be bounced from pillar to post. The university's goal is to provide our students with the highest level of support, even as it teaches them how to navigate university policies and processes so they can do so on their own. CSU-Global considers this part of a student's education and applicable to situations they will find in the workplace and in life.

ACHIEVEMENT

Growing numbers of Americans with some college but no degree, $1.3 trillion in federal loan debt, and the projection that 65 percent of all jobs in 2020 will require postsecondary education—all of these facts make it abundantly clear that higher education needs to become part of the solution rather than perpetuating the problem.

Students at CSU-Global enroll to be successful in attainment of their personal, academic, and professional goals. In many cases, it took a lot of courage for them to return to school, so the university ensures that students have all the resources needed to complete a degree or certificate program or other academic goals. Student academic and workplace success is the university's success, so CSU-Global measures that achievement. The university's multipronged strategy for doing so is unique in higher education and keeps the university and its personnel accountable.

For example, CSU-Global's spring 2017 data show that one year after graduation, 94 percent of CSU-Global 2016 alumni agree that their program helped them achieve their professional goals. That's a far cry from the mere 6 percent of graduates nationwide who strongly agree that their education prepared them for workplace success. One-quarter of CSU-Global alumni also receive a promotion within a year of graduation, and, according to third-party credit bureau reports, their salaries have continued to rise each year since we began measuring this with the first 2012 graduating cohort.

Businesses that employ our alumni are pleased, as well. A full 98 percent of employers are satisfied, or very satisfied, with the performance of CSU-Global graduates in their employ. They rate their graduates high on the learning outcomes identified for each of the university's degree programs; on the soft skills of written and verbal communication, problem solving, collaboration, and ethical behavior; and on use of technology, leadership, and organization and planning.

HELPING STUDENTS SUCCEED

CSU-Global's highest outcome is its student's success. Each of the following chapters highlights one important way in which the university makes that success possible.

While most higher education institutions would deny it, they are in the product and service business. Faculty and staff are providing instruction and courses as the product, and assistance and support as the service. Like any service provider, if they are going to be successful in today's dynamic environment filled with distractions and other education options, they must define what will make them successful. It is customary for many academic institutions to measure their success against one another. But if their peers are equally unsuccessful in specific areas, such as student graduation rates, then institutions that compare their own bad results to others' equally poor performance may not understand that they have significant problems. CSU-Global rejects that line of thinking, which is why it measures itself by its own mission and goals, as high-lighted in the next chapter.

2

DEFINING
SUCCESS

By definition, innovators have no peers, so they must
determine their market, design their product, and define
their own metrics of success.

Think Amazon or Southwest. These market-driven companies are now household names, but when they began,
they had existing market competitors but no real peers.
They identified a niche and responded with transformational products, innovative delivery methods, and
exceptional customer service. Because each is in business to thrive and to adapt their industries to address
modern-day consumer needs, they have adjusted their
products and services as their consumers' expectations
have changed.

CSU-Global could be considered akin to such innovators. Being the first fully online university created to meet the needs of nontraditional learners has provided the institution with the freedom to create methods and models that best serve students in today's technology-enriched environment. Because the university is free from traditional institutional constraints, and because it does not receive state funds (while also reporting to the same board as its sister campuses), CSU-Global has evolved to be a high-quality, self-sustaining, and fiercely student-focused institution that is still able to offer students tuition rates that have not increased in more than six years.

The university is clear that its mission is to provide high-quality academic programs to empower students to be successful in the workplace. As such, CSU-Global is continually evolving to meet the needs of a new generations of students and emerging workplace trends. It has evolved beyond its standard eight-week online courses. Today, the university offers programs in competency-based education, unique types of scholarships that encourage student engagement and retention, career coaching, tuition planning, and student experience departments that help students understand what going back to school will mean for them as individuals. Even as the university surpasses industry benchmarks in such areas as student retention and graduation rates, CSU-Global's only true measure of success is the extent to which it is meeting its vision and mission: *to ensure the workplace success of its students and alumni through their university experience.*

BENCHMARKING TO PEERS: A RACE TO THE BOTTOM?

Imagine if this were the private sector. Businesses would never judge their success based on the fact that their competitors are similarly inefficient or addressing a shrinking consumer base. Successful businesses must offer products and services the public wants and provide a return to their stakeholders, or they will be forced to close their doors. In education, students are investing in their futures. As educators, we have an obligation to do our utmost to facilitate student academic achievement toward workplace success and provide a return on their investment. It is not enough for us to benchmark to the status quo, where only 30 percent of students graduate in six years' time.

I came to CSU-Global with academic qualifications, but I was primarily an experienced business person. So, when I was tasked on my initial arrival in 2008 with developing a list of institutions that were similar to ours, I was comforted by the opportunity to do something that was familiar to me. I conducted a SWOT analysis, used by organizations to identify internal strengths and weaknesses and external opportunities and threats, and I prepared to present the information to the other university leaders. What I discovered surprised me.

My detailed SWOT analysis did not impress anyone. Instead, I learned that everything in higher education is evaluated relative to peer institutions, rather than based on the possibilities of what any one institution could potentially achieve. For example, colleges and universities compare their retention rates to those of their peers, not to absolute goals to retain and graduate students.

On returning to the university in 2009, it became my mantra that every student who walks through our doors has given up their hard-earned money or taken out a loan to be at school, and every student that starts a degree or certificate program or signs up for a course usually has the intention to finish it. So, the fact that a student drops out is a problem we must address, regardless of whether a peer institution faces a similar dropout rate. I understand there will be attrition in everything that requires longitudinal commitment. But we can't accept the status quo as an acceptable target. What happened to striving for excellence, just as we expect our students to do?

This same philosophy of benchmarking to their peers guides higher education institutions in myriad other ways.

College and university overhead and compensation costs are heavily weighted to what peer institutions are paying, versus what a particular institution can actually afford based on its enrollment and other sources of revenue. For CSU-Global, especially in those early years without state funds as a backup, it was less about what peer institutions were paying their staff and faculty and more about what the university could afford, including my own salary. Back then, we devoted whatever resources we had toward services for student success, and, even today, we will spend a dollar on our students before we spend a nickel on ourselves.

Through the years, I have continued to find it interesting that even small, nonprofit state institutions mail an avalanche of four-color, glossy brochures about their institutions to each other, not strictly to possible alumni donors and grant makers, even when those funds could be used toward student-success initiatives. I understand that the reason I receive such mailings is that they are timed to sway the peer-to-peer voting that is included in institutional rankings programs, but if CSU-Global only had $1,000 left in its coffers, it would use those funds toward its student-support resources and not toward influencing its rankings. The institution believes in its mission, which is firmly rooted in the fundamental values that contribute to the success of CSU-Global students, society, and the nation; it is the university's student-based outcomes that matter.

Like all educational institutions, CSU-Global is required by the federal government to supply certain data, including information on the number of students enrolled; pass, fail, and withdrawal rates; types of courses and programs students are enrolled in; student demographics; and retention and completion. The university's data meet or exceed those of other schools. But if all institutions aim to have data that match their peers—meaning they are all offering the same type of product or service with the same outcomes—why do we need so many of them?

CSU-Global is a relatively new university with its own independent accreditation and a singular mission: *to prepare nontraditional learners for workplace success in a global marketplace through education.* University personnel believe the sky's the limit for CSU-Global students and alumni and for themselves, but to maximize that opportunity, they know that they need to do far more than simply meet or exceed industry benchmarks or peer data. CSU-Global has a responsibility to its students to define their success as its own success and not to rest until that goal is met.

The success of companies like Amazon rests in part on their ability to sense what the market needs at any point in time and to change or expand their offerings in response. Amazon is a provider of goods and services; CSU-Global is a provider of higher education toward workplace success. That gives us a wealth of avenues to explore, and we do it the same way Amazon does, by looking to our customers. The institution examines student behavior, collects data, and makes changes designed to better serve student needs.

CSU-Global knows that its "customers" are nontraditional students. They are working and caring for their families, many are first-generation college students, and a significant percentage are from diverse backgrounds. Some of CSU-Global's students are making the transition from the military to the civilian workforce. The university has created an environment to prepare all these students for workplace success.

That's why CSU-Global is an online university. We can provide education face-to-face but, when we tested that delivery method, we found that students don't engage. The university's students need the flexibility to attend classes on their schedule, not CSU-Global's. They want or need the support they receive from the online environment.

University personnel also know that the demographics of the student population are changing. When CSU-Global was first launched, it was serving Baby Boomers and members of Gen X, and those individuals are very different from students in Gen Y, otherwise known as the Millennial generation. Each generation has different ideals, values, and expectations, and they have different knowledge of, and comfort with, technology.

Now CSU-Global has a whole new generation—Gen Z—that will be coming to it soon. University personnel will watch how these students behave in class, how they complete their assignments, and how well they achieve their goals. If this newest cohort of students is not succeeding with the infrastructure and processes CSU-Global has in place, the university will make changes. CSU-Global is never stagnant. It doesn't just build it and think it's done. That's not how companies like Amazon innovate, and that's not what this institution does. In fact, while some institutions develop five-year strategic plans, CSU-Global develops plans that look no more than two to three years ahead. This allows us to be on the leading edge to meet our students' needs and expectations, while incorporating new tools and resources to be efficient and effective at meeting university goals.

For example, in recent years, CSU-Global has begun

offering internships, and it is examining the possibility of including international exploration trips. But, as with everything the institution does, such offerings will be tied to its mission and its students' goals. CSU-Global health care administration students may study what it's like to provide health care in a country with universal access and coverage. And we'll measure what students learn to offer credits for student experiences. Such initiatives take work-based education to the next level, and CSU-Global is in pursuit.

ENSURING OUR NATION'S FUTURE

As a nation, we need to prepare workers for today's economy. People who lost their jobs in the last economic downturn have had trouble reentering the workforce because they don't have the education and skills to fill jobs that have different requirements.

Technology has also sped up the rate at which businesses operate, and those companies that are thriving have adopted processes and procedures that require skilled workers. Factories no longer need individuals to assemble products by hand—they need employees who can operate the technology that drives the machines that are doing the work. They need workers with the critical-thinking skills to troubleshoot problems and the technical skills to fix them.

Without an educated, savvy workforce, we risk becoming a nation of haves and have-nots—of individuals with good-paying jobs and those who can't even find low-end jobs because so much of the work has been automated. Think of open-road tolling that has replaced tollbooth collectors, self-pay machines that have replaced parking attendants, and, at some point in the not-so-distant future, self-driving cars that will replace taxi and Uber drivers.

At CSU-Global, driving toward academic and workplace success for its students and alumni is not just its passion. It's about ensuring our survival as a nation.

As a fairly new institution with a modern way of thinking about its students and its criteria for success, CSU-Global strives every day to improve its data on student retention, graduation, and workplace achievement. The university has surpassed industry benchmarks, and it has identified an abundance of metrics to help ensure that the work it does meets its students' needs. CSU-Global doesn't believe in peer parameters. Instead, we have a boundless view about how the university can execute on its mission to best serve its students.

The bottom line is simple: The better institutions get at defining their markets and doing a really good job of serving them, the greater their chance of success. Today's students demand the Amazon experience in everything they do—they expect transformational products, innovative delivery methods, and exceptional service that meets their individual needs. And higher education can give it to them.

VALUE FOR THE MONEY

As savvy consumers, today's students are very intentional about how they spend their time and their money. They want to be certain they are getting the best value in education. To meet their expectations and our goals, CSU-Global delivers. In the next chapter, we look at how the institution ensures that its students have a return on their investments.

3

RETURN ON INVESTMENT

———

Even young children understand the value in getting something for their time and their money.

In the summer, kids everywhere want to have a lemonade stand. They excitedly go about making sales signs, finding the right-sized tables and chairs, and begging their parents to buy or make lemonade for them to sell. They eagerly set up their stands and sit outside for hours at a time, hoping to sell out. After a couple of hours, if they have not sold any cups of lemonade, or at least not enough to buy something they want, they pack up, head home, and vow never to do it again.

The lesson is clear. Children don't set up a lemonade stand

just to hand out a cool drink to their thirsty neighbors. They want to earn money. They may even put up some of their own money if their parents insist that they use their allowances to purchase supplies. When the lemonade doesn't sell, they are out both time and money. They conclude that selling lemonade is a bad investment.

This same scenario plays out every day in higher education. We see increasing numbers of individuals, more than 44 million at last count, with some college, but no degree.[1] They are out both time and money, with nothing to show for it.

We see college graduates who are unemployed or underemployed. These individuals went to college, got their degrees, and then ended up without a job or taking jobs that do not require the cost and time of earning a degree. They spent both time and money, but their investments didn't pay off. They could have gotten the same jobs without going to college.

We see college graduates who are unprepared for work. Marketing students fresh out of college are expected to write press releases, but they didn't learn how to write press releases in college. They learned about the theory

---

1   "Educational Attainment," United States Census Bureau, March 2017, https://factfinder.census. gov/faces/tableservices/jsf/pages/productview.xhtml?pid=ACS_15_5YR_S1501&prodType=table.

of the Four *P*'s: place, price, promotion, and product; or they learned about consumer behavior. But they didn't learn about how to execute the actual activities that take place in a marketing department.

Even at CSU-Global, the university expects its employees to come with job-ready skills, but typically they are not "plug and play." They may have learned how to think and make decisions from a theoretical perspective, but not how to negotiate media buys or respond to negative press or unfriendly blogs—those things they learn in the workplace. When I studied economics at UCLA, I learned wage theory and supply-and-demand theory, but not how to research and negotiate salaries in the real world of work.

That paradigm is not going to fly in today's fast-paced, technologically driven work environment, and it's not going to pass muster with today's nontraditional students. For the 75 percent of students who are nontraditional learners, higher education is only part of their lives. They are juggling school with jobs, family responsibilities, and community service. For them, going to college is not a luxury; it's *an intentional decision with a specific goal*—the ability to get a job that pays a living wage or to advance in their careers. Like the kids running a lemonade stand, they expect a return on their investment, and CSU-Global delivers.

Times are very different in this country than they were ten or twenty years ago. College has become more expensive, and even families who might once have been able to afford a traditional four-year college education for their children are tightening their belts. The most recent recession had a lot to do with this. Everyone is more aware of the value of a dollar.

At the same time, we've seen an influx of immigrant families. They came to this country, worked hard, and established themselves. Now they want their sons or daughters to attend college, but those children are also working in their families' restaurants, and may even be working additional jobs to contribute to the family income. If those children go away to school for four years, even on full scholarships, they become unable to help provide for their families.

Today's students and their families are very intentional about how they spend both their time and their money. They look to institutions like CSU-Global because the traditional model of higher education does not work for them. Students can't start at point A and automatically expect to enter a job at point B; a traditional four-year academic degree is no longer a golden ticket to employment at a living wage.

When I think about all the colleges and universities that are out of business or being forced to close their doors, I believe their lack of sustainable enrollment is due to the fact that many are offering the same experience to students. Many institutions say, "Come one, come all." But without differentiation, there is likely a lack of return on investment, because no institution—whether brick-and-mortar or online—can be all things to all people. At a time when individuals can choose the color of their tennis shoes or the specific type of song they want to download, offering the same experience to very different individuals is a recipe for intense competition and easy failure.

Think again about the lemonade stand. Maybe it was an unusually cool summer day, and potential customers would have preferred hot chocolate. CSU-Global doesn't offer degrees and certificates to those who would prefer trade school assistance. Its brand promise is to provide its students a return on investment based on a singular value proposition—*workplace success measured by salary increases or the ability to change careers.*

How does the university ensure workplace success? CSU-Global selects degree and certificate programs, hires faculty, measures learning outcomes, conducts surveys on alumni and employer satisfaction, and tracks salaries so that every CSU-Global graduate can say with confidence that they got what they paid for. It's not difficult, but it does require intentionality.

DEGREE PROGRAMS FOR TODAY'S INDUSTRIES

CSU-Global chooses its degree programs based on research that shows which areas of employment have growth potential over the next decade. University faculty and staff examine whether the industry is growing, whether it pays a living wage, and whether the salaries and growth potential are sustainable and able to support CSU-Global alumni.

The institution is very deliberate about which programs it adds or removes based on these market trends. For example, in 2017, CSU-Global added a bachelor's degree in management information systems and business analytics because the university's industry research and experts identified that those skills are and will continue to be in high demand at relatively high salaries. The need for people who can use technology to manipulate and evaluate "big data" will only continue to grow. Even CSU-Global senior staff are interested in getting a certificate or degree in this up-and-coming field.

Conversely, the university discontinues degree programs if it finds that demand slows or wages fall. Based on its mission, CSU-Global doesn't allow its students to do the course work and pay tuition if university research reveals they are unlikely to be able to get a job or earn a living wage in a particular field. Each year, the institution surveys the global marketplace and identifies opportunities to add or discontinue programs, or to convert them into specializations that pair with degrees in more lucrative fields, such as business management, accounting, and technology management.

To help university personnel make these decisions, CSU-Global uses industry data from commissioned research entities, which aggregate job openings across the country. It also has services that allow its students to search for careers by such variables as city, state, skill set, title, and pay. For example, CSU-Global has a system that allows students to learn for themselves that there is a big demand within an identified pay range, in a specific city, for IT professionals who have a certain set of skills and level of experience. Then students can decide on their own or with help from a CSU-Global career coach how to pursue this opportunity.

The university makes this type of information available to its students for free because it wants them to be intentional about choosing their careers. A student who wants to pursue a degree in criminal justice and a specialization in cybersecurity may find there are no openings in their hometown for someone with that expertise. This student might need to move to a bigger city or a different state if this is their chosen career. CSU-Global students can use this information to pursue degrees that meet their interests and skills, and that allow them to choose where and how they live.

FACULTY WHO KNOW THE ROPES

CSU-Global prepares students to be successful in the workplace. To do so, 90 percent of its faculty have work experience in their respective areas of expertise, and 84 percent have bona fide expertise based on their doctoral degrees. This hiring methodology helps faculty relate to students' problems in the workplace because they practice what they teach.

This has very practical implications. Members of the CSU-Global faculty serve as career coaches so university students can have discussions with them that go well beyond theory. Perhaps an IT student is having difficulty communicating effectively with a superior, or a human resources major is trying to get promoted and needs advice. Their instructors and coaches can offer advice based on their real-world experience.

In addition, because CSU-Global students are working,

the university creates communities of learners who can help one another. Instructors regularly see in their classrooms that students are providing advice and counsel to other students on work challenges. The camaraderie evident in CSU-Global's online classes helps students translate what they learn to workplace success.

This real-life collaborative learning is invaluable to CSU-Global students. If they have a conflict with their bosses, or they want to know how to get a promotion, they can talk to someone who has had that experience. This CSU-Global environment is very different from my dad's university experience or from mine, where I sat in the back of the five hundred-person auditorium and listened to the lecture before getting up and moving on to my next professor's class.

REAL OUTCOMES FOR REAL ACHIEVEMENT

Because faculty at traditional academic institutions plan their own courses, they also determine their own teaching methods, required textbooks, and learning outcomes. CSU-Global faculty and curriculum development specialists build courses with standardized grading rubrics that allow for multiple sections, while helping ensure consistency in grading and standardization of outcomes. This means that despite the inevitable variability of instructor styles and perspectives, the actual learning concepts are uniformly delivered, tracked, and measured.

At CSU-Global, as we'll see in the next chapter, data drive everything we do. The university is very intentional about the data it collects and about how it uses this data to evaluate the performance of staff, faculty, and students.

The university is not merely satisfied with students who are happy or who receive good grades. We want to know with granularity and specificity what our students have learned, what level of competency they have achieved, and what their perceptions are on what they have learned, so we track student-learning data and survey them in every class. If students are not learning what CSU-Global faculty believe they should be, faculty examine the courses and learning objectives and refine course information and activities accordingly.

In particular, because all CSU-Global work is online, the university can use an electronic system to track student learning and outcome achievement. For example, as faculty members assess student papers, CSU-Global technology operating in the background aggregates the faculty scoring in real time to record whether students have achieved specific learning outcomes, including demonstration of critical thinking. This allows the university to determine the level to which individual students have achieved designated learning objectives.

The institution can also determine how all students performed as a whole. If students are not meeting learning outcomes, CSU-Global can examine what went wrong. Were the students having difficulty understanding the material? Was it the course instructor for that particular section who did not teach the material well? Or did the outcomes not correlate with the learning activities? CSU-Global goes back and refines the classroom information and activities so that learning objectives and student achievement align. This is how the institution promotes its goal of helping students to be academically successful and workplace-ready.

CSU-Global knows that today's students have choices. They can go to traditional academic institutions and get a broad understanding of the world. They can go to technical schools and learn specific trades. Or they can come to CSU-Global and *be prepared for workplace success in a global marketplace through higher education.*

SURVEYING SUCCESS

Every academic institution conducts student satisfaction surveys, and CSU-Global is no exception. The university wants to know whether its students are pleased or unhappy with their experiences, what they think they have learned, and whether they would recommend the institution to friends or family members. More than 30 percent of CSU-Global students are from referrals.

Every year, the institution also surveys its alumni. CSU-Global wants to know how helpful their degrees have been in specific areas, such as leadership, collaboration, and use of technology. Equally important, we want to know whether alumni are advancing in their careers as measured by salary increases. Between fiscal years 2013 and 2016, CSU-Global graduates self-reported salary increases of between 17 percent and 19 percent since graduation.

The university also researches salary by graduating cohorts. It provides cohort information to a major credit reporting agency, which delivers aggregated data on graduates' median salary, specific to each degree program. The extrapolated longitudinal data are used to examine graduating cohort's salaries when they begin at CSU-Global, when they graduate, and every year thereafter. The most recent research confirms a continual and steady rise in salaries following graduation.

Finally, CSU-Global surveys the employers who hire its graduates, and if employers identify weakness in a specific area, university personnel go back to those degree programs and individual courses and make content changes to better facilitate student knowledge for their success. As noted previously, 98 percent of employers are satisfied or very satisfied with the way CSU-Global graduates perform, based on their specific degree program's learning outcomes. And the accompanying chart reflects the fact that employers are satisfied with our graduates' demonstration of the critical and soft skills that employers have identified as important to the workplace. This is further supported by self-reported information directly from CSU-Global alumni.

Surveys of Employers

Employer-identified Skill for Workplace Needs (AASCU Hart Research, 2015)	Percentage of Employers that report that their college grad employees are well-prepared (AASCU Hart Research, 2015)	Percentage of Employers of CSU-Global grads that report that their CSU-Global grad is performing *Extremely Well* or *Very Well* (CSU-Global Fall 2015 & 2016; N = 128)	Percentage of CSU-Global grads that *Strongly Agree* or *Agree* that their CSU-Global education provided the identified skill (CSU-Global Spring 2017; N = 637)
Working with others in teams	37%	90%	72%
Current on technologies	37	90	83
Ethical judgment/decision-making	30	91	93
Oral communication	28	92	69
Written communication	27	91	94
Critical thinking	26	94	95
Analyzing/solving complex problems	24	87	N/A
Working with people of diversity	18	86	89

DATA-DRIVEN EXCELLENCE

CSU-Global believes that it owes its students a return on investment of time and money. If students leave without earning a certificate or degree or completing the courses they intend to take, they are out both time and money. This means they are worse off than if they had never enrolled at all.

What CSU-Global does is not magic or rocket science. It is, however, based on intentional efforts to reach lofty goals, supported by constant streams of data that help the university continuously improve everything it does for its students. The university collects standardized data, continuously interprets it in real time, and uses it to drive quality improvement. The next chapter examines its use of data in more detail.

4

DATA IS NEARLY EVERYTHING

—

Years ago, if you had wanted to drive from Denver to Los Angeles, you might have purchased a paper map and marked your route, noting any planned stops along the way. Today, you are likely to punch your destination into your car's navigation system or use an app on your phone. You might select your route based on shortest distance or fewest tolls. The one thing you would *not do* is just get on the road and hope you arrive at your destination.

Likewise, earning a degree or certificate is a journey, one that requires markers along the way. Students need to know which route to take, and faculty and staff need to know how to guide them. Institutional stakeholders need to understand whether the coordinates they have plotted lead to the destination; if not, the map needs to be redrawn. Just as GPS technology allows drivers to determine the best route based on their destination, such advancements as adaptive learning and predictive analytics mean that learning can be customized, facilitating success toward a predetermined goal.

CSU-Global maps its students' progress toward workplace success and its own objectives toward university excellence, every step of the way, and it uses data to help it do so.

CONNECT THE DOTS

Students begin college with a goal: to graduate, to earn a certificate, or to complete courses that will provide the specific information they need. Yet, as previously shared, just over half of Americans who start down this road never arrive at their destination. Data can help us change that.

I learned the importance of data when I worked in Macy's executive buying program, fresh out of college. You don't buy a certain sweater because you think it's fashionable. You buy it because the collected stores' data show that one color or style sells at a faster rate than another color or style. For example, as a buyer, the data can tell you that you have a better chance of selling out a collection if it has red cotton sweaters in it instead of blue silk sweaters. Similarly, we have a better chance of preparing our students for workplace success if we have the data that show us what tools, resources, interventions, faculty, and advisors contribute to student success.

But it's not just raw numbers we need—every institution of higher education collects some type and level of data. The keys to success are twofold. First, colleges and universities must collect data that *begin and end with the student*—from who they are and what they should be studying to whether they are succeeding, in class and on the job. Second, academic institutions must use this data to *connect the dots*. At CSU-Global, we are continually asking the questions that will aid in our work to help our students succeed. We do so by creating real-time research studies based on hypotheses that we test to search for challenges and opportunities.

Let's consider a typical scenario at more traditional academic institutions. Suzie Kwon enrolls in a degree program, which has been designed by a faculty member. Will the program Susie enrolled in help her find a good job when she graduates?

Suzie starts classes, but stops showing up. Why did she stop coming to class? Her professors report her absences to the institution's department coordinator, and, eventually, that information makes it to the registrar. Do the professor and the registrar coordinate with each other to share the information they have about Suzie? Is she succeeding in the other courses she is taking?

Separately, Suzie sees her student advisor and mentions that her mother is ill. Does her advisor circle back with Suzie to see if she has reregistered for the classes she is missing? When information on her poor grades reaches the financial aid office, staff report that Suzie's scholarship is in jeopardy. Do they check with the registrar to see why her grades are slipping?

Who is asking the critical questions about Suzie, if staff in separate and siloed departments don't share the data they have? If they are sharing information and asking the right questions, they should be able to help Suzie overcome what ideally should be a temporary setback. But without support to help her reach her goals, Suzie likely drops out of school, with no school official to reach out to her to ask why or how they can help her return.

If the goal of institutions is to graduate students, why would we let Suzie drop out? Why aren't we asking the critical questions, about Suzie and about every student we serve? We must understand whom we are serving.

We must assess how well we are serving them. We must determine how we can serve them better.

CSU-Global doesn't have 100 percent retention, but it does work hard to ask the critical questions, and it collects data that help provide the answers. More important, the staff and faculty are empowered to *work together* to use this information to steer individual students toward success. They use data to continuously improve courses and degree programs and the support services the university offers. CSU-Global's work begins and ends with its students.

REAL DATA FOR REAL SUCCESS

CSU-Global's mission is straightforward: *to prepare nontraditional learners for workplace success in a global marketplace through education.* And its students' goal is equally direct: to succeed in their chosen profession. To help meet its mission and its students' goals, the university measures seemingly everything about its students, gathering data on its potential success in preparing them, from before they enroll to after they graduate.

The institution asks questions, gathers data, and connects the dots so that the students have a real chance at success. University personnel know the demographics and numbers of new students each month, the percentage that stay enrolled beyond the third term and from trimester to trimester, and which students are not engaging in the classrooms. The university also knows how many credits students transfer into their programs, from which institutions, and the history of similar students and their success rates. The data are continually analyzed and applied toward new and revised processes, policies, and initiatives to intentionally drive higher levels of student engagement, retention, and academic goal completion.

Importantly, the university annually secures its alumni salary data based on graduation cohorts. CSU-Global tracks the median salaries of its graduates, beginning with their first year after their graduation and every year thereafter. As shown in the accompanying graphs and chart, the university can also see historical salary medians by cohort going back three years before they graduated. This type of data helps CSU-Global measure its impact to help ensure that it has focused intentionality around tools, services, and curriculum that promote students and alumni workplace success.

Equifax Income Trends by Graduation Year - *Bachelor's Degrees*

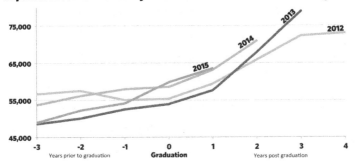

Equifax Income Trends by Graduation Year - *Master's Degrees*

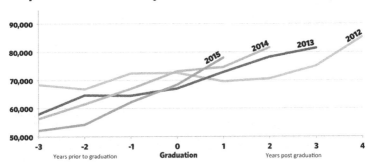

CSU-Global Alumni vs. National Average

Type of Graduate	National Median*	CSU-Global Alumni 1st Yr ^	CSU-Global Alumni 5th Yr ^
Bachelor's degree	$ 59,124	$ 61,061	$ 79,370
Master's degree	$ 69,732	$ 70,488	$ 92,880

* U.S Bureau of Labor Statistics March 2016
^ Equifax Fall 2016 Graduate Outcomes Report – 2010 and 2011 completion cohorts

Because CSU-Global wants to leave its students in a more competitive position than when they started, the university must understand what they need to learn.

All incoming undergraduate students take a third-party nationwide assessment, which they retake when they are getting ready to graduate. We see from the accompanying data, which reflects the incoming and outgoing scores of each student, that CSU-Global students, on average, grow in the key areas of critical thinking, reading, writing, and mathematics.

ETS Proficiency Profile	PRE		POST		Increase in Percentile
	Score:	Percentile:	Score:	Percentile:	
Total Score	442.18	68	445.93	81	+13
Critical Thinking	115.5	60	113	89	+29
Reading	117.98	61	118.81	75	+14
Writing	113.6	37	114.18	63	+26
Mathematics	112.54	53	113.16	73	+20

Includes 310 CSU-Global students with Pre and Post ETS Proficiency Profile data, from incoming cohorts Fall 2010 – Fall 2015, and completer cohorts of FY11/12 – FY16/17 Fall Trimester.

The Percentiles - National School Mean represents the distribution of institution scores and subsequent percentiles, and includes 155 institutions and 222,846 students participating in the ETS proficiency profile from July 2010 to June 2015.

Overall School Percentile Score
Percentile to the National School Means Fall 2016

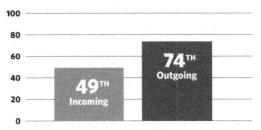

National Educational Testing Assessment Scores for CSU-Global students against an entire test population of 222,864 students from 155 degree-granting institutions.

Comparison of National Schools Mean Percentiles for CSU-Global incoming students vs Fall FY17 Fall trimester graduates.

Relative to the more than 222,000 students who also take the assessment, graduating CSU-Global students' assessment scores place them in the seventy-fourth percentile in critical thinking, reading, writing, math, humanities, social sciences, and natural sciences. But what is more impressive is that, based on matched-pair data, the students demonstrate measurable growth in learning, up from just the forty-ninth percentile when they start at CSU-Global to the seventy-fourth percentile when they graduate. While the university does not measure itself on peer data, it does measure its success by the fact that its students are progressing significantly in key areas during the time they spend with us.

CSU-Global is focused on grooming its students for workplace success, so it must determine that what they are learning is what the university set out to teach them.

At traditional academic institutions, learning outcomes are typically determined by individual faculty members for the courses they teach. CSU-Global takes a more intentional approach by developing its learning outcomes in collaboration with its faculty—who have industry experience in their fields—and with the industry experts who help it design its programs for workplace readiness. The university builds learning-outcome measurement into all its courses, and it tracks the data in real time.

For example, as a faculty member is grading student assignments, he or she uses CSU-Global's technology-driven learning-outcomes measurement system. The instructors see the grading rubric on the screen, and, as they are marking the points that a student earned and adding comments, the system electronically calculates student performance toward designated learning outcomes. The university wants to understand at what level students achieve designated learning outcomes. This is a measure of its success.

The university can also tell on an assignment basis, for

individual students and for the class as a whole, whether students achieved the designated learning outcomes agreed to by the faculty and industry experts. If the students are not achieving at least an 80 percent score at the undergraduate level and 85 percent at the graduate level, institutional personnel ask themselves a number of questions. What did we intend to teach them? What did the assignment request? Did the course content and our expectations align? If not, what can we do in the class to close the gap going forward?

At the end of each course, students and faculty receive a survey that asks them to evaluate the course, highlighting its strengths and weaknesses. The data are captured and used to refine program offerings further.

REAL FOLLOW-THROUGH

Because CSU-Global intends for its students to finish what they start, it aggressively tracks student retention, including retention in specific courses, first-to-third term retention, and trimester-to-trimester retention. If our hypothetical student, Suzie Kwon, enrolls at CSU-Global, *we are fiercely determined not to let her fall through the cracks.*

If Suzie doesn't finish a class, or doesn't register to attend the next class, we will know that. We can see immediately on a per-course basis if Suzie isn't participating each week, because we can see whether or not she's logging in and participating in a discussion-board activity, or whether she's submitting assignments. Automated alerts go to the university's student advisors, who will follow up with Suzie to see if she needs help.

CSU-Global also examines data on all the support services that are designed to help Suzie succeed. Are she and her classmates using our twenty-four-hour, seven-day-a-week live tutoring services or our library for this course? At what time are they using the library? If most usage occurs after 10:00 p.m. on weeknights, do we have enough staff at that time to help students find what they need? Do we have enough tutors, and are they available when our students need them? The university tracks this data and uses it to make changes.

At CSU-Global, administrative staff and leadership are also held to equally high standards. Are staff members responding to student communication within twenty-four hours? Does the data reflect that students are getting the help they need? If not, why not? The university has an integrated database for student communication and complaints that tracks student contact with staff, so everyone can see who responds to a student's concern, how quickly staff act, and how the issue is resolved.

CSU-Global's mission and our students' goal is for them to graduate and be successful at work. The data can tell us if the students are having a problem, but we have to *use the data* to determine what the problem is and try to fix it by *connecting the dots!*

COMING FULL CIRCLE

CSU-Global doesn't stop collecting or using data once its students graduate. As previously noted, the institution surveys alumni about their job satisfaction and their salaries. It also surveys alumni employers about their satisfaction with their CSU-Global graduates. It gathers third-party data about compensation for graduating cohorts to compare this information with alumni self-reported salary increases. This data helps the university determine what degree programs to offer, bringing us back to where we started at the beginning of this book.

All of this data is available continuously to create reports that staff and faculty access. The data are given to task forces, committees, and departments that convene regularly and repeatedly to diagnose challenges. Faculty, staff, and administrators use the data to design, implement, and improve organizational processes that allow the institution to move its students forward on their journeys toward workplace success.

If what CSU-Global does seems overwhelming, I'm here to tell you it's not. It's more overwhelming to operate in the dark. As a business person, I can't imagine operating without the level of data we collect. As an educator, I can't imagine not using the data to guide our students toward success.

CSU-Global personnel are always asking questions. Who are the students? What do they need? Why do they behave the way they do? How can the institution serve them better? They are researchers in action.

Many institutions of higher education conduct extensive research on various subjects for a multitude of reasons, and that can include intentionality around student success. Their own institution, their data, and their students provide a rich environment for learning what works, making some changes, and evaluating the results.

There are about seven to nine such experiments going on at any one time at CSU-Global. The university tests its hypotheses with small experiments, examines the results, makes modifications, and tests again before it increases the size of the experiment or moves to scale. It may take several revisions to the experiment's original structure, but the university tries to make sure that it has exhausted the possibilities before it discards them and implements a completely new experiment to try to address a specific challenge.

When CSU-Global makes a big move, it may appear to come out of the blue. But it's likely that we have spent years collecting and analyzing data to determine whether this move makes sense given our mission. In other words, we first toss a pebble before we throw a stone, and after seeing the results, we know when it's time to launch a boulder.

For example, when CSU-Global decided to offer competency-based pathways for students to earn credit, it started with competency-based exams and created the syllabi for a couple of test courses. The institution effectively "tossed the pebble" by providing the exams to just a handful of students enrolled in the standard eight-week courses to see whether what they learned in their courses would ensure that they passed their competency-based exams.

After many faculty meetings with psychometric test experts and exam redesigns, the university was able to successfully achieve that goal, so it "threw the stone" and began offering the new competency-based syllabi and exams to students who were not exposed to the standard coursework. Once additional modifications were made to study resources to achieve satisfactory passage rates, the institution then "launched the boulder" by offering competency-based resources and exams for the majority of its undergraduate courses. It was a more than two-year journey of nonstop testing, data evaluation, and constant improvement, and it was rewarding when one of CSU-Global's students completed his bachelor's degree at a cost of about $15,000 because of his access to competency-based credits.

Every college and university across America can do the same thing. They can, and many do, collect the data that tells them who they serve. They can use the data to design programs that get results. They can share the data with faculty, staff, and administration to make student success an institutional goal where *everyone is held accountable.*

Is the marketing department attracting the students they know, based on data, will retain the course information and be successful? Is the curriculum department developing courses that will help students graduate and find jobs or meet other university goals? Is the financial aid department ensuring that students realize that what they take out in loans needs to be repaid with interest, thereby helping them understand what the real cost of their education will be?

Others frequently ask CSU-Global how they can achieve these results. The answer is not complex, but there are multiple questions that need to be answered. What do your data tell you about who your students are and what they are seeking by attending your institution? What do your learning outcomes by class and by program tell you about your student achievement levels? Are your alumni satisfied with their college education? What do they believe was helpful, and does that correlate with the data on what they were seeking from your institution as students? In sum, there must be intentionality about asking the questions and using data in order to explore the alignment of student outcomes and expectations to verify student success.

THOSE THAT CAN, TEACH

There is an old saying in education that goes something like this: "Those that can, do. Those that can't, teach." CSU-Global has turned that saying on its head. The institution's data reveal that students want and need to learn from those who have real-world experience, so it has hired experts who are both academically qualified and active in their fields to help design and teach its courses. The many benefits of this approach are highlighted in the next chapter.

5

FACULTY AND ADMINISTRATION

———

Today's college graduates are considered by many to be ill-prepared for workplace success, because when they enter their first jobs out of college, they do not have workplace-ready skills.

Think about how you shop for expertise. If you need heart surgery, you will look for a physician who has performed the same or similar surgery many times. You will likely shy away from a surgeon who has just earned his credentials and has only been in the operating room as an intern. In similar fashion, we want our attorneys, electricians, and accountants to have real-world experience.

If experience in the field of medicine or law matters to

us when choosing our surgeons or our attorneys, why would we behave differently when selecting higher education instructors? These are the individuals charged with providing our students with the information and skills they need to succeed at work. Only having academic credentials isn't a bad thing, but having both an academic background and hands-on industry experience provides for richer and more engaged student learning.

NO SUBSTITUTE FOR EXPERIENCE

I saw this in my own life. When I was studying for my MBA, my classmates and I all wanted to get into the marketing class that was taught by a guy who was an advertising executive by day and a university instructor by night. Like all of my instructors, he assigned textbook reading, but during class he shared client stories to explain how theories applied in real-life scenarios.

For example, he could tell us what to do if, despite all our research and planning, a client wanted to do the opposite of what we recommended. The complexities of managing that scenario, to arrive at a decision that an agency could support and that the client was willing to pay for, was fascinating and certainly not in the textbook. I looked forward to every single class, and I worked hard to make my homework assignments worthy of his time to review. I was thoroughly and totally engaged.

Conversely, my graduate school instructor in finance taught us about currency exchange, but he had never been a currency trader or held a Wall Street position; he had chosen the academic route to become a tenured professor. When a student asked him a question about how markets might shift in response to a recent world event, he could tell us what he expected might happen based on the theory and past history. Yet, he had no personal examples to draw on to further engage us. He was clearly very smart and knew his history and theory, and he could explain currency market dynamics, but the lectures were just academic, making a difficult subject even more challenging.

As a baseline, university faculty members typically need at least a master's degree, if not a doctorate. Most tenured faculty members, however, have spent a majority or all of their entire careers in academia, writing journal articles and conducting research in their field.

If a research university is graduating students who are all expected to become researchers, it makes sense that these students would be taught by people who have been researchers. Or if students are enrolled in education courses, having instructors who have been in academia most of their professional lives adds value. At CSU-Global, the faculty members who teach in its master's of science in teaching and learning classes fit this bill. However, because the institution is preparing people for the workforce outside of research and education, it believes it needs faculty who have actually worked in their areas of expertise in organizations beyond academia.

A HIGH BAR

The Gallup poll data shared earlier reveal that the vast majority of college graduates don't feel that their studies adequately prepared them for work. And many employers are dissatisfied with recent graduates who, though they have been taught by well-educated people, have little idea what to do when things don't go as the theory predicts.

When I was an intern at IBM, many future employees were trained over time before reaching a hire/no-hire decision, but today's employees are expected to be able to do a job on day one. Businesses can't afford to have their employees immobilized by problems. Employers need people who can make decisions on the fly, roll with chaos, and find a new path forward.

CSU-Global hires faculty members who can help its students learn these skills, and who can also share their own stories of overcoming organizational chaos. These practical examples and stories of overcoming adversity and unforeseen challenges provide CSU-Global students with an additional view of what really happens in the workforce to ready them for workplace success.

The university has set a high bar, and few meet it—CSU-Global accepts only 6 percent of those who apply to teach. And as a university within a research system, CSU-Global understands the importance of academic preparation. Currently, 84 percent of university instructors have a doctorate degree in their field. All courses are based in research theory, but the institution makes it relevant and applicable to its students' everyday lives, which is why a full 90 percent of the faculty have industry work experience in their areas of expertise.

In many institutions, part-time instructors who are also working in their fields teach a course or two at night to fill gaps in a school's offerings. They are largely left on their own to plan and teach their individual classes. Most of CSU-Global faculty members are part-time, but the university requires extensive, ongoing training. Faculty participate in all curriculum development and revision activities and on task forces and committees in every area of the university. In recognition of their time and effort, the university pays them stipends to acquire training, and it also compensates them for their participation in various ongoing and ad-hoc university initiatives.

As with everything CSU-Global does, the search for faculty is quite intentional. The typical instructor has earned his or her academic credentials later in life, but is working in their area of expertise or has done so for many years. Often, they are teaching as a way to give back to the community. Their experience plays out in the classroom in much the same way as it did in my graduate school advertising class.

For example, when I teach a leadership class, I assign reading on the theories of various leadership styles, which can be rather dry. I then discuss some of our most notable US leaders, and, as a class, we discuss what type of leaders they are or were, based on the theories we've learned. I also share examples of my own past bosses and my leadership style. I can kick it up a notch by pointing out ways in which, for example, Steve Jobs was a transformational leader. I can tell my students that I have worked for people as intense as Steve Jobs and give them my personal thoughts on how they might want to respond if they work for such a leader.

My students can take this information and apply it to their

own lives. They can identify specific leader types at their jobs, or in their churches or community groups. They can determine what type of leader they are or aspire to be, and we can discuss their thinking in the online discussion boards, by telephone, or face-to-face through video technology. Student assignments also align with these real-life, critical-thinking exercises, and, as I score them, the learning-outcome tracking technology records the level of achievement students demonstrate.

CAREER COACHING

Our faculty's real-world expertise is critical, because not only do they teach in class, but they are also trained to serve as career coaches. CSU-Global students have free access to forty-five-minute sessions with our faculty career coaches.

Career coaching provides CSU-Global students with one-on-one mentoring in specific situations that they may encounter in the workplace. The university knows that after graduation, about one-quarter of its students change careers. If a student wants to move into a career in IT, he or she can ask a career coach who works in IT what type of interview questions to prepare for.

Even CSU-Global students who are happy in their chosen

field hope to advance in their careers. They can ask a coach, who is a leader in their chosen field, for insights on what it takes to move up the career ladder.

Outside of formal coaching, we see students and alumni reach out to their instructors for workplace-related assistance. Often, students post discussion-board responses that garner feedback from both their peers and their instructors on how to tackle on-the-job problems or even troubleshoot technical issues.

A DIVERSE APPROACH

CSU-Global serves nontraditional learners, so it intentionally employs nontraditional faculty—those who are not lifelong academics. The university also deliberately matches its faculty to the demographics of its students.

With 40 percent of CSU-Global students being first in their families to attend college, and nearly one-third of the students coming from non-Caucasian, diverse US populations, CSU-Global works to provide equal percentages of faculty from these same populations. It may seem counterintuitive that, in a virtual environment, it's important to hire faculty who look like the students or who share similar life experiences. But it's precisely *because* the institution is an online university—where much of a student's experience is built on the relationships they have with faculty members—that matching CSU-Global students with faculty who are like them is critical for student success.

For example, CSU-Global works with students from low-income communities who may not have the support from family and close friends to attend college. A number of the university's faculty have been in similar situations. They understand that having support from an instructor or classmate can make the difference between a student remaining in school or becoming discouraged and dropping out. The faculty can provide this level of support and understanding for the students and direct them to additional resources to help them succeed.

The university also actively seeks to hire faculty with military backgrounds to serve its students who are active military members or veterans. And because the faculty represent its students, CSU-Global includes faculty on every committee and task force and involves them in budgeting and strategic planning. Without their diverse backgrounds and views, which mirror those of its students, CSU-Global would be far less successful at understanding how best to serve its students, and how any proposed changes in its policies and procedures might affect the ability of students, alumni, and employees to succeed.

A WORKPLACE-BASED MODEL

Learning from faculty who are working in the trenches is not the only way to gain practical experience. High schools, and an increasing number of colleges, embrace an apprenticeship model in which students receive credit for working in a business in their chosen field.

In a typical college or university, a student might be able to do an internship in lieu of one or two classes during their four years in school. Students are given an outline of what they're required to learn, assigned a direct report to verify that they learned this information, and awarded academic credit.

CSU-Global offers students credit for internship and practicum programs, and it holds these programs to the same high standards as all its offerings by creating standardized learning outcomes and surveying students, faculty, and employers. The university is also collaborating with education, government, and business leaders in Colorado to study the Swiss apprenticeship model, which offers students a combination of work- and classroom-based instruction. From our data, we know that when students learn both theories and skills that are relevant to their everyday lives, they remain engaged and are more likely to graduate and be successful at work.

Internships and apprenticeships are a further way of uniting the education and business communities to fill a gap in the talent pipeline, and also to engage some students who would otherwise drop out of school due to lack of interest in the traditional higher education paradigm. Just as an oil or gas pipeline sends natural resources where they are needed, we must, as a nation, send workers who can fill positions in business that help secure our competitiveness at home and abroad.

This is not a new concept in education. Postsecondary vocation schools have long focused on offering students the ability to apprentice, one-on-one, with skilled craftsmen. Around the world and over the years, these apprenticeships became known as the "university of tailors, of smiths, and so on." Land-grant universities had their heritage in agriculture and mechanical arts—education created to facilitate the production of crops for food and to build industry.[1]

Over time, student interest in apprenticeships declined as the then-modern version of higher education evolved to deal with large groups of students returning from World War II. In this model, students were expected to take

---

1   Committee on the Future of the Colleges of Agriculture in the Land Grant University System, Board on Agriculture, and National Research Council, "History and Overview of the Land Grant College System," in *Colleges of Agriculture at the Land Grant Universities: A Profile* (Washington, DC: National Academies Press, 1995), 1–17, available at https://www.nap.edu/read/4980/chapter/2.

college-preparatory classes in high school, enroll in good colleges, get their degrees, and find high-paying jobs with benefits.

Over the last decade, when students and their families began to realize that their investments in higher education were not guarantees to job attainment at living wages, scrutiny of the system began. Today's students don't fit the "standard mold" mentality. They want individualized services, and they want to know that what they study will translate into workplace success. This is why CSU-Global hires faculty who are leaders in their fields to teach and mentor its students.

We are coming full circle, offering students the chance to study with those who are skilled craftsmen in their trades. But now, instead of learning how to be blacksmiths, CSU-Global students enter the world prepared to be human resources executives, health care administrators, and IT professionals, among many other career paths.

WHERE THE RUBBER MEETS THE ROAD

Lack of time and lack of money are the two key reasons students disengage from higher education. By hiring faculty who can prepare CSU-Global students for work, in classrooms that are designed for students to take what they learn today and apply it at work tomorrow, the university ensures that its students' time is well spent.

But, as with most decisions made in our consumer-driven economy, the cost of a college education is where the rubber meets the road. If students can't afford to be in class, they won't come. If higher education can't guarantee up front what their certificates or degree programs will cost, then students may not stay to finish their education or meet their goals. The next chapter examines how CSU-Global makes college affordable and predictable to the students it serves.

6

MONEY AND TIME MATTER

———

We are trained to be savvy consumers with an eye on the bottom line, and paying for higher education should be no different.

Every January, people who make a New Year's resolution to get in shape flock to their local gym. They may be lured in by a low introductory rate, so they ask questions about when and by how much the membership cost might increase. They want to know whether there are additional fees for other services or amenities, such as hot yoga classes or use of the pool.

Potential members also consider their own fitness or weight-loss goals and how long they might continue to use the gym. If costs rise annually, they may evaluate their progress in light of their original goals and decide to cancel their membership. They might even shop for a new gym and find one that better fits their budget or their new requirements.

Every spring, when high school students receive mailings from traditional colleges and universities around the country, they begin asking the same types of questions. How much does tuition cost? What about student fees? How much will these costs increase each year? Will I be able to afford to graduate? Students and their families need this information to make an informed decision about what, for many, will entail a significant financial sacrifice.

Unfortunately, most schools can only begin to answer these questions. They may be able to tell students what tuition and fees will be for the first year, but they can't guarantee that costs won't increase, and they can't say by how much. In fact, we know that between 1986 and 2015, tuition costs more than doubled, outpacing inflation and putting costs well ahead of median family income.[1] There is little transparency in how tuition and fees are calculated, which makes it even more difficult for students and parents to forecast costs and budget appropriately.

---

1   Jennifer Ma et al., "Trends in College Pricing 2016," College Board, 2016, accessed July 9, 2017, https://trends.collegeboard.org/sites/default/files/2016-trends-college-pricing-web_1.pdf.

We know that time and money are the two key reasons that students disengage from higher education. We can't necessarily help students arrange the time to go to college, but we can and *we must* help make it affordable.

AFFORDABLE MEANS ACCESSIBLE

CSU-Global's goal is to help students graduate and be successful at work, so it gives them every reason to stay and complete their degree. The university's financial policies are transparent. It sets its budget based on its tuition, not the other way around. The university also provides guaranteed tuition and pay-as-you-go pricing. It offers institutional loans and a variety of scholarships, and it also offers no-interest payment plans to maximize the available options that meet the individual needs of its students. As with everything done at CSU-Global, the university makes college affordable because *it begins and ends with the student.*

A BUDGET THAT SERVES STUDENTS

Most traditional academic institutions develop their annual budgets to uphold their status quo. Brick-and-mortar institutions have much greater physical infrastructure to maintain than does CSU-Global. Buildings, some of them centuries old, need regular maintenance, and that part of the budget is fairly rigid. But many colleges and universities adopt a similarly inflexible mindset when it comes to budgeting for faculty and staff. They set their budgets based on their fixed overhead costs *and* on what they want to pay their staff and faculty. Then, they adjust tuition and fees to cover those seemingly fixed costs.

This isn't how budgeting is done at CSU-Global. We believe costs are flexible. We begin with the previous year's tuition rate, project the number of continuing and new student credit hours and associated revenue, and subtract costs per credit hour for all academic and student-support services. We add any additional costs needed for strategic initiatives that facilitate our mission.

CSU-Global locks tuition for individual students for the length of their programs, and it offers all student ser-vices—including career coaching; twenty-four-hour, seven-day-a-week tutoring; and library resources—at no additional cost. In 2018, the university will mark its sixth consecutive year without a tuition increase. To achieve this, it continually looks at ways to be more lean and effi-cient, which we'll examine in the next chapter.

The bottom line is simple. CSU-Global budgets based on what its students need; that's where its money goes first. The university's goal is to retain and graduate its students so they can be successful in the workplace, so all financial decisions begin and end there.

MANAGING TUITION COSTS

The tuition planning process at CSU-Global is rigorous and transparent. The university wants students to know, before they start classes, what their entire certificate or degree program will cost. This helps them budget for their education and allows the university to help fill in the gaps.

Before students start their first class with CSU-Global, they meet with a tuition planner who helps create an enrollment agreement that specifies how many credits, if any, can be transferred toward degree completion (versus credit accepted for "transfer" but not actually applied toward degree completion, a common practice at other institutions);[2] how many credits students must complete for the degree they choose; how much those credits will cost; and, if they are using federal funds, how much money is left in their lifetime allotment of federal assistance. The process helps students understand the true financial costs of their education and helps them figure out how to manage those costs in a way that works for the student and the university.

---

2   See chapter 8 for information about our transfer policies, which is one way we are able to reign in tuition costs.

CSU-Global also guarantees tuition for every student who is continuously enrolled at the institution. Students pay only for the courses that they need to graduate on a cost-per-credit-hour basis, rather than paying a set tuition cost over a specific time period, such as a semester. The university figures out the number of credit hours and the classes that students need to graduate, outlines the associated costs in their enrollment agreement, and then never raises that cost while students are actively taking classes through to graduation.

Compare this to double-digit tuition increases at some traditional colleges and universities. If a student has to pay several hundred dollars more a month in tuition, along with student fee increases, they may decide partway through their degree program that college is no longer affordable. Now they have nothing to show for their time or their money. If the goal of educators is to provide students with a college education, they must identify innovative ways to create a win-win relationship between institutional and student success.

PAY-AS-YOU-GO PRICING

CSU-Global's pay-as-you-go pricing models also include two lower-cost options for completing student coursework. One model is the competency-based education (CBE) program.

The concept behind CBE is simple. Students identify a specific course in which they want to demonstrate their level of competency through an assessment, rather than by participating in one of the standard eight-week classes. The university provides students with free resources for a self-paced, self-taught course. Students do the readings and complete the practice assessments, and, when they think they're ready to complete the course, they pay $250 for two opportunities to pass a proctored exam.

The cost the institution charges covers the proctoring conducted by webcam, so that students can be monitored while taking the exam, and the time of the faculty who grade the exam. If the student passes the test on the first or second try, they are awarded the designated credits. CSU-Global's passing rate, including those who take the exam a second time, is about 72 percent.

This is different from other universities where students pay a flat fee for a specific period of time for the chance to earn an unlimited number of credits. Graduation rates at one of the largest institutions that follow this model are below 20 percent,[3] in part because self-directed, competency-based learning isn't for everyone, especially those students with

3   U.S. Department of Education, "College Navigator," National Center for Education Statistics, accessed July 9, 2017, s.v. "Western Governors University," https://nces.ed.gov/collegenavigator/?s=all&q=western+governors+university&id=433387.

weaker academic skills and self-motivation challenges. CSU-Global doesn't want to take a student's money up front when there's a chance they will never complete the course. The institution is clearly focused on saving its students money *and* helping them succeed.

GSU-Global students who have on-the-job experience may also choose to do a prior learning assessment (PLA). Here's how it works.

The majority of courses at CSU-Global include a final portfolio project. Students conduct research and demonstrate their knowledge by writing a research paper or giving a presentation. The grading rubric is well defined.

Students who qualify for PLA complete only the course's final portfolio project. They don't pay for access to the standard eight-week classes. The only cost is $150 to submit the project for faculty review, and, as with CBE, they have two chances to succeed. If the student's initial attempt doesn't line up with our grading rubric, they can rework their project and submit it a second time. When students receive a passing score, they are awarded the requisite number of credits for the course.

This is especially helpful for the university's older students and those with work experience that aligns with their degree programs. Perhaps they've been a supervisor or a manager for twenty years, and there is an Introduction to Management class that is required to complete their degree. Students can examine the learning outcomes and the grading rubric for the final assignment and apply to get into the PLA program. This speaks not only to the university's goal of keeping costs low, but also to the value CSU-Global places on lifelong learning.

FINANCIAL AID

Once we know what a student's education will cost, we help the student figure out how to pay for it. Staff in the tuition planning department examine whether the student qualifies for any of the various federal funding programs to help cover some of their costs. The university also has its own institutional loan program with a lower interest rate than what a student could get from a bank or other commercial lender. But it doesn't stop there.

The university has more than five hundred affiliate partners, from government agencies to large and small corporations that offer discounted tuition to their employees who are CSU-Global students. Our affiliate partners appreciate the flexibility of a 100 percent online education—their employees can study on their own time and use what they learn in the classroom to improve on the job.

In addition, each trimester, CSU-Global students can apply for scholarships to cover the cost of their studies that term. They fill out a one-page application to indicate why they are an appropriate match for one of these awards, including those given for academic excellence, financial hardship, career advancement, community service, and military service, among others. The university also helps students find scholarships provided by various corporations and organizations in their communities.

In 2015, CSU-Global began piloting a new type of scholarship that helps students minimize the amount of student loan debt they incur. For students in good standing who are enrolled in a degree program, the university provides scholarships to reduce the cost of a standard year of classes, and then reduces the cost of the classes in the student's final trimester. The data reflect that CSU-Global is retaining these students and that they are performing well in class. We believe it's in part because these students have "skin in the game." The scholarships help discount the cost of their education, but it's not free.

NO FREE LUNCH: WHY STUDENTS NEED TO HAVE "SKIN IN THE GAME"

As a public, nonprofit university, CSU-Global would like to be able to give every student a "free" education. The idea caught on during the 2016 presidential campaign and is being considered by several states. But the data the university has been collecting for years are clear: Students whose education is fully paid for don't do as well academically and don't graduate at the same rates as students who are shouldering at least part of the costs, through loans or by paying out of pocket. CSU-Global students who have invested in themselves are more likely to carry through on their commitment to attend classes and earn their degree.

Think back to the gym membership. People who pay to exercise may be more likely to follow through with their fitness goals than those who keep saying they will get up in the morning and run. In our society, many things that are free aren't perceived with the same value as those that require us to part with some of our hard-earned cash; hence, CSU-Global has found that its students' behavior mirrors the popular saying, "You get what you pay for."

In fact, even if the cost of college is fully covered, there are built-in requirements that mean it's not really free. Where else would you get something for nothing and then have to do all the work to realize the benefits? We see this with the massive open online courses (MOOCs). Such courses are typically free, and individuals can take as many or as few as they want, but completion rates are low. MOOC students must strive to learn on their own, wait to see if their questions are ever answered, and then may have to pay for exams to earn college credits. This is not an experience the majority of CSU-Global students could thrive in; therefore, the university continues to provide the customized experience its students need and want.

THE SIMPLEST PATH IS THE BEST

Enumerated cost projections. Guaranteed tuition. Pay-as-you-go pricing. Transparent budgeting. CSU-Global's policies align with its overall mission to graduate students who are prepared for workplace success. To offer an affordable and, therefore, accessible education, it minimizes its administrative and overhead costs. The university is always looking for ways to be lean and efficient. But this doesn't just help CSU-Global students afford college. It also helps them navigate the college environment more smoothly than if we sent them hither and yon in search of what they need to succeed. The next chapter explains how and why CSU-Global aims for simplicity and efficiency.

7

EFFICIENT AND READY FOR SCALE

Simplicity, connectedness, and accountability are what we have come to expect in any product- and service-based experience, and higher education should be held to these same standards.

When I plan a vacation, I go online and check the flight options. I can find the flight times that best fit my needs. If I want to use my accumulated miles, I can indicate that in the search, and then I can decide between paying for the flights or using miles. I can then choose the seats I want for each flight segment, and I can book the flights—all in a matter of minutes. If, instead, I had to call an airline agent to understand my flight options, speak to another agent to see if I could use my miles in lieu of cash or credit, and speak to yet another agent to secure my seats, the journey to my vacation has suddenly become complicated and time-consuming, and I might decide to stay home or just drive to a closer destination.

The more time and inconvenience it takes to reach a goal, the more likely we are to choose another path or give up on the goal altogether. I've seen this in higher education firsthand.

Recently, I wanted to enroll in a food-science class at an established university. I thought it might be a fun way to learn something new. The university required that I show up on campus, and I spent nearly a full day there. I went to several different places because they were confused about what to do with a non-degree-seeking student. After I finally signed up for the class, I went to another office to pay. From there, I waited in line at the bookstore to get my textbook and culinary kit, and then in another line in another department to get my parking permit. Thinking about signing up for another class is daunting, based on the time it takes to get through the enrollment process alone. I've decided to find a different path to learn the skills I seek.

CSU-Global *puts its students first*. Nontraditional students are working and caring for their families. The university wants them focused on their studies, not on operational logistics. We do everything we can to streamline our processes so that our students can smoothly enter school, take classes, and move to the next term, all while gradually learning what it takes to navigate the university on their own. To graduate students who can succeed at work, CSU-Global focuses on simplicity, connectedness, and accountability in pursuit of excellence. Every institution of higher education can do the same.

KEEPING IT SIMPLE

Getting a college degree can be stressful enough without having to worry about fitting the pieces together. When I visit college campuses, I see various rooms and service windows with titles on the doors and students standing in line. Every door or service window and every line is meant to address a particular student issue.

That system can be effective in solving a distinct issue, such as a problem with payment. But if a situation involves more than one department, the student is sent running from one window and building to the next, much as I did in attempting to take my food-science class. When this happens, the student is the one who acts as a liaison between the various departments, but that's not their job. Their job is to learn. CSU-Global helps students navigate the complexities of higher education as painlessly as possible so they can focus on learning.

Each potential student works with an enrollment counselor who helps the student submit required entrance documents, coordinates the transfer credit process, and introduces the student to our tuition planning department to create the student's enrollment agreement. Enrolled students are then assigned a student advisor who can help a student with all future needs.

The student advisor keeps tabs on the financial aid team's work on behalf of each student, works with the registrar to arrange a student's leave of absence or other course registration issues, and willingly and patiently answers any and all questions a student might have. Much like the airline website, CSU-Global student advisors work in the background to coordinate responses from multiple departments on the student's behalf. By removing the logistical headaches, the university strives to mitigate frustration and achieve a high level of student satisfaction. Most important, given the university mission, CSU-Global retains and graduates students at levels above the national norm.

None of this implies that CSU-Global believes its students are incapable of navigating a college environment.

In fact, as the students learn the ropes, they rely on their advisors less over time. But the university has learned that CSU-Global students get the most out of their tuition dollar when they are not spending time chasing after pieces and parts that are not related to what they're here to learn.

CONNECTING FOR SUCCESS

At brick-and-mortar institutions, the enrollment department, financial aid department, and student advising department typically are in separate buildings. CSU-Global has the same departments, but they are all in one building. Students can work with the staff by telephone or online, rather than running between departments. However, that's not what makes the difference to our students. What sets CSU-Global personnel apart is their dedication to connecting the students to what they need by *connecting with one another*.

For example, if a CSU-Global student is having a problem in class, the student advisor examines that student's situation in the class. The advisor may reach out to the instructor to discuss any problems. If needed, the advisor may connect the student and instructor to try to resolve the issue together. All of this can be done in a traditional environment.

Separate buildings are an explanation but not an excuse for lack of coordination on traditional campuses. If staff in the enrollment department pick up the phone or send an email to staff in the financial aid or student advising office, the student in front of them won't have to run to two or three buildings to get their needs met.

This is no different from booking that airline ticket. It would be frustrating for me to call three different numbers to book and pay for my flight, and students shouldn't have to go to three or more buildings to enroll in classes and pay their bill. CSU-Global respects its students' time by streamlining its internal processes, which are designed to ease the administrative burdens of higher education.

ACCOUNTABILITY IS KEY

Even the physical plant and staffing structures at CSU-Global are designed with our students in mind. The university's infrastructure design saves money and holds everyone accountable for student success.

The university keeps costs low by housing all administrative and staff offices in one building. Because some staff work remotely, university personnel share office space—every cubicle and every office can accommodate at least two people, and some have space for three or four.

Staff and faculty connect to one another easily because they share the same space, use technology easily and instantly to virtually connect with one another, and because there are no gatekeepers. CSU-Global has no secretaries or administrative assistants. This helps keep overhead costs low, but, equally important, it makes clear that faculty and staff members are accountable directly to each other. The university is not managed by secretaries and administrative assistants but by department personnel who talk and work with each other to efficiently achieve their individual and departmental goals.

Without additional layers of staff surrounding them, CSU-Global faculty, staff, and administrators remain connected to one another and to the students. University personnel come together quickly to make decisions and respond to student needs. All faculty, staff, and administrators are hands-on at CSU-Global. Contact information for senior leadership is in the student portal, and students can call or email even the president or provost directly with questions or concerns.

The university's mission is to educate students for workplace success, and it considers its faculty, staff, and administrators to be leaders in that arena. As such, CSU-Global expects them to be on the front lines, keeping tabs on student needs and implementing policies with transparency and speed to ensure student success.

CSU-Global knows that scalability of what it does is important so that it can serve increasing numbers of students. The university looks to outsource work when it will provide equal or better outcomes at a lower cost, and it relies on technology to help fill in the gaps. The sheer dynamics involved in growing both vertically and horizontally are not for the timid or weakhearted.

Importantly, the internal structure and processes at CSU-Global are seamless and invisible to the student. Students concentrate on learning, graduating, and excelling at work, and the staff and faculty concentrate on everything that makes that possible.

PURSUING EXCELLENCE

CSU-Global continually strives for excellence because our students' success is our success. Through simplicity, connectedness, and accountability, the university ensures the smoothest possible experience for its students, but it doesn't do their work for them. Faculty and staff set high standards for the students, and they measure students' ability to be successful before they enroll, while they are students, and after they graduate. If CSU-Global students are coming up short, university personnel take a hard look at themselves, as we'll discuss in the next chapter.

8

LEARNING FOR REAL LIFE

———

Being successful in school, at work, and in life requires competence in any number of skills, but competence is difficult to demonstrate simply by taking a test.

When we want to get a driver's license, we take a written test that assesses our understanding of what certain road signs mean, what the rules of the road are, and what to do in less than ideal driving circumstances. We may practice driving in a simulator. We also get behind the wheel of a real car and drive while an evaluator checks off the various requirements of good driving. Getting our first driver's license is an exercise in competency.

During my first year at CSU-Global, a colleague of mine

suggested that what I needed to do to be successful in leading the institution was to take a popular fourteen-day course in higher education process. This confirmed my belief that in traditional higher education, process seems to matter more than outcomes in judging competency. Prospective college students submit standardized test scores to enroll in school, and then take innumerable multiple-choice exams on their way to graduating. They may get good grades, but none of this confirms whether a student will finish their degree and succeed at work.

The rigidity of sticking to processes simply because "that's the way it's always been done" is indefensible in a world that has dramatically changed. As a newer university, CSU-Global has a different lens. The university emphasizes outcomes over process, and, when considering students for enrollment, it looks at both demonstrated grit and grades. Grades are important, and CSU-Global students work hard to complete courses or work toward their degree or certificate program. But their ability to finish what they start and to apply what they learn are the yardsticks we use to measure success, because *student success is our success.*

GRIT AND GRADES

CSU-Global can accept students with previous credits for

transfer, but for those without previous college experience, the university must abide by state regulations on freshmen acceptance, which means it reviews students' standardized test scores. However, for all its students, CSU-Global doesn't just evaluate test scores or student grade-point averages (GPA). We also consider student work history and their reasons for wanting to attend the university.

CSU-Global has a required entrance GPA, but in a world of inflated or inconsistent standards in grading across institutions, the university can also take into account potential student work performance and motivations for enrolling. We can assess whether potential students have what it takes to stick with school and finish their degree or other academic goal. We don't want students to give up their time and their money and not reach their goals.

Students can have a high GPA or a great SAT score, but that doesn't necessarily mean they will be successful at CSU-Global, so the faculty and staff look at whether the students have "grit." In other words, can they stick with something over time? Whether it's a job, a club, or a volunteer activity, have they invested in something and stayed with it?

Often, the university encounters students who have a high GPA, but they've switched jobs every six months. Those signals convey that these students are likely to be intelligent or smart enough to know how to get good grades, but they may have difficulty maintaining their motivation to complete a bachelor's degree program that requires 120 credits, or a master's degree program of thirty-six or more credits.

Conversely, CSU-Global has the ability to send students who don't meet its stated entrance requirements to the university's provisional admittance committee. This committee reviews everything it has collected on the student before it decides to admit them or decline their applications.

CSU-Global personnel may also look carefully at students who have low GPAs. Such students might have attended college right out of high school, not committed themselves to their school work, and never finished. The university doesn't hold potential students' histories against them; instead, faculty and staff want to see what these students have done since that time. Maybe they secured a job and consistently advanced in their career, from line worker to manager to director. That demonstrates tenacity to succeed.

In fact, CSU-Global recently had an applicant who was a vice president of a very large technology company who hadn't finished his bachelor's degree. He may not have been accepted at a traditional institution because his GPA was too low. But we saw the determination with which he moved his way up the career ladder, which demonstrated his commitment to learning. The university admitted him, and he was a solid student who graduated without issue.

Going to school is not easy. Even if it's online and convenient to their schedule, students still have to participate in class, submit homework, and complete the course. There are no points for just showing up. CSU-Global sometimes has students come to it from other colleges and from for-profit educational institutions that have different academic standards than we do, but we see from our data that, over time, these students are able to rise to the university's standards and excel.

CSU-Global offers all the support necessary for students to be successful, including student advising, technical support, adaptive learning environments, one-on-one tutoring, and career coaching—all at no additional cost. But if students aren't willing to put in the effort it takes to be successful, the university is firm that it can't compensate for their lack of grit.

If the focus across all of higher education were on outcomes rather than process, it would make it easier for colleges and universities to accept transfer credits toward degree completion.

CSU-Global doesn't require that students learn everything from us. The university does require that students demonstrate they have met our faculty-approved learning outcomes for the courses they want to transfer. When the institution accepts transfer credits toward degree completion, it passes up the opportunity to earn additional tuition, but revenue is not the priority. *This is about CSU-Global working in the best interests of its students.*

The university strives to be as outcome-based as possible in accepting credits from other institutions. History classes are a good example. If a student has studied world history prior to 1945, the content of that class will likely be similar to what CSU-Global's courses and instructors provide, because the subject matter hasn't changed. What's important is whether the learning outcomes for that class match the learning outcomes CSU-Global has for the same class. If faculty determine that the outcomes are the same, and the student has successfully met these outcomes, the university can accept the transfer credit. This is an easy way to help make college affordable and save students valuable time. Why should they pay again to study what they have already learned?

The university also considers experience earned on the job and in the military. Many businesses, from McDonald's to Hyatt, offer management and leadership training. Members of the military receive training in their occupational specialty and, often, in leadership. CSU-Global faculty examine the syllabi for these trainings. They review the learning outcomes and whether students show evidence of having met them. They may also determine whether the trainings have been vetted by the American Council on Education, which evaluates workforce and military training that demonstrates college-level knowledge and competencies.

However, regardless of whether others have judged a specific training program to be comparable to a college course, the faculty are very intentional at CSU-Global about awarding alternative credits. They can do so only if they determine that students demonstrate learning the way the institution defines and measures it. The university doesn't want to graduate a student who cannot be successful in the workplace, because that's our final benchmark. No one is doing the students any favors if the university tries to save them a few dollars, only to have them lose out on getting a lucrative job after they graduate.

CSU-Global works to ensure that it accepts those students who can be successful at the university because it has high expectations for them.

Faculty and staff understand that students can study to a test and get good grades, but that doesn't necessarily mean they have what it takes to come home from work, log in to their classroom, and start their next assignment. Students who have been successful in the workplace have demonstrated that level of commitment. In addition, all our classes, assignments, and discussion-board topics relate back to the workplace.

Because CSU-Global wants its students to be on par with their colleagues, it teaches them the same theories and research they would learn at other reputable colleges or universities. But its students are working and want to advance in their current job or change careers, so workplace-focused learning is included. A number of CSU-Global students are also studying to qualify for industry certifications.

The university asks its students to demonstrate their knowledge and share it through workplace-based assignments. Students take the theory they are taught; test it in the workplace or in the community; and then write a paper, draft a case study, or participate in a laboratory simulation. CSU-Global's goal is to have students reveal how theory plays out in the real world. This requires a higher level of critical thinking than just taking a test, and it aligns with how the world actually works—an added real-life educational benefit beyond the classroom.

The same level of critical thinking is required of CSU-Global faculty. There is very little in the way of conventional testing at CSU-Global, which means its faculty don't just feed a multiple-choice exam filled out in No. 2 pencil into a machine that spits out a grade. The university's grading rubric requires that students can demonstrate successful application of the theories they've learned, that they can competently conduct and apply research information, and that they can effectively integrate and communicate their findings. Because faculty members serve as mentors and career coaches, they must provide feedback geared not just toward helping students get a good grade, but also toward helping them be successful in the workplace.

The faculty also monitor class participation. The university's online classrooms have an average of 15 undergraduate students and 9 graduate students, and instructors expect a response to every single discussion question they pose. They review class input and provide feedback online or in one-on-one sessions with individual students. As highlighted previously, student learning by course and by program is tracked electronically.

This is very different from my experience as an undergraduate, sitting in lecture halls with hundreds of students. The professor stood at the front of the room and reviewed the reading, and a few students participated. After class, students headed to the bookstore, bought the lecture notes, and studied for the exam based on the notes.

Also, students in physical classrooms who miss a few lectures can quickly fall behind. Perhaps they were stuck in traffic, got sick, or had a big deadline at work. They can do the reading and consult the notes, but they have little sense of what the instructor is emphasizing.

It's more difficult for students to disengage in our online learning environment. If they miss a live lecture session, they can watch the recorded session. They read the course lecture, hear the instructor present the materials, and read or hear the instructor's responses to the questions posed by their fellow students. Though they missed the opportunity to ask a question in real time, the university's students can email an instructor or post a question to discussion boards at any time and expect an answer within twenty-four hours.

Monitoring outcomes doesn't stop when CSU-Global students graduate. The university needs to be able to prove with confidence that its graduates can be successful in the workplace, which is why its employer and salary surveys are critical.

When the university initially began surveying employers, it was surprised to learn that many employers felt CSU-Global graduates were weak in their understanding of diversity and leadership skills. We expected no less than 90 percent of employers to be satisfied or highly satisfied with our graduates in these two areas, so we tackled the issue with task forces, additional surveys, and workgroups.

The faculty and industry advisors reworked instruction in those areas and developed assignments that allowed students to apply what they were learning about diversity and leadership to the workplace. They revised the grading rubrics to ensure students demonstrated the new learning outcomes. The university's most recent employer surveys show that 89 percent of employers are now satisfied or highly satisfied in those two areas, which means we're on the right track toward reaching our goals.

CSU-Global also continues to monitor student salaries by examining longitudinal data on graduating cohorts over a period of five years. The university's 2017 data from the class of 2012 indicated that salaries continued to increase, though not by as much as in previous years. Technology and globalization require an increasing cadre of skilled workers, which speaks to the need for lifelong learning. The university's salary data support that trend.

SUCCESS FOR ALL

Every student who comes to CSU-Global has given up their time and their money, and they expect to graduate and be successful at work. Though the university exceeds industry standards for retention, it still loses roughly 15 percent of students by the end of the third term.

CSU-Global competes against itself, and losing 15 percent of its students is not an acceptable benchmark. Even if students take only one class—paying $1,050 for an undergraduate class or $1,500 for a graduate class—that's real money out of their savings or added to their loan balance, and the university believes they are owed a return on their investment.

That's why, at CSU-Global, *students come first*. We define success based on our own metrics, and we regularly collect and parse our data. We hire faculty who are working in their fields, cap tuition, and keep a lean and efficient infrastructure. We emphasize outcomes over process.

CSU-Global is doing well in moving toward achieving our mission, but because American competitiveness depends on having a skilled and educated workforce, we look forward to the growth of other universities that share our mission and workforce views. In the conclusion that follows, we'll examine what all of higher education can learn from the university's success.

CONCLUSION

WHAT COMES AFTER

Every successful organization, large or small, responds to changing marketplace demands, and higher education must do the same—not just to survive as an industry, but to help restore American competitiveness.

Let's revisit the lemonade stand I introduced in chapter 3. With a goal of making money, our young entrepreneurs eagerly set out their wares and waited for customers to arrive. If they were successful, they may have decided to set up again the following Saturday. But maybe it was a cool or rainy day, and folks passed them by. Perhaps the children concluded that they should have offered hot chocolate instead, or added cookies to sweeten the deal. The next time they set up their stand, these lessons will help them determine how to reach their goal. If, however, they continue to offer lemonade to customers who prefer hot chocolate, their model will prove to be unsustainable.

This story is more applicable to higher education than one might think. In my early years as president at CSU-Global, I met a fellow university president at an industry association meeting. He bemoaned the fact that his student enrollment had been steadily declining. He explained that he was unable to reverse the decline, because he didn't have faculty with the expertise needed to create or teach the subjects students wanted to study. Instead, he was trying to find a market for the programs that the faculty had developed based on their areas of expertise.

Suddenly, I understood clearly one of the fundamental challenges of higher education institutions today. Fitting a product to a market, rather than identifying the needs of the market and offering a product to fill that need, is a losing proposition. It's one thing if a business does this and has to close its doors. Few people suffer when there is one less clothing store.

But when the business is higher education, and colleges and universities close their doors, our citizenry's future and our nation's economic health suffer. America needs a skilled, educated workforce to retain its standing in the world, and higher education has a responsibility to adapt to meet these needs. The success of CSU-Global proves that this is possible.

EVOLVING TO MEET CHANGING DEMANDS

American higher education is struggling to keep pace with a changing world.

The factory model of higher education that evolved in the wake of World War II was set up to educate the masses, with the expectation of jobs at the end of the conveyor belt. Today's reality does not match this decades-old expectation.

Today's consumers expect *choice, transparency, service,* and *achievement.* They seek choice in everything from their running shoes and their music to the food at their favorite restaurant. They want value for their money, individualized service, and a sense of achievement. They expect no less when they enroll in college or sign up to take classes, and higher education can deliver.

Colleges and universities have the ability to provide different outcomes for different markets, and they must do so if they are going to survive into the future. While we have seen smaller and for-profit institutions close their doors over the past decade, relatively few institutions are immune to the possibility of closure. Trillion-dollar student loan debt, changing demographics, negative public perception about the value of higher education, and declining state funding across the nation put the higher education industry at risk.

Yet, it seems that, rather than make the difficult decisions to terminate programs and close departments that lack sufficient student support and enrollment, college and university leaders prefer to let government officials and other stakeholders determine their future.

Even more mystifying is the lack of understanding that merely matching revenues to expenses is no longer good enough. New concepts, new designs, and new ways of operating have real costs in the short run. But these investments are crucial to sustaining the future of higher education, and leaders may have to bite the bullet as we did when I rejoined CSU-Global in 2009. We cut operating expenses to seed the programs and services that addressed our students' needs. Even today, we identify our year-to-year efficiencies as we make room for new, if not costly, innovation that benefits our students.

Often, I hear parents complain that their twenty-eight-year-old children earned degrees and are still living in the basement. They blame the college or university their children attended, but, though I understand their frustration, I think their anger may be misplaced. If their son or daughter attended a liberal arts college that promised to broaden their child's mind and enhance their critical-thinking skills, that school may have delivered fully on its promise. The problem is that critical thinking divorced from the realities of today's fast-paced, technologically driven global marketplace doesn't necessarily ensure employability.

With more than half of college graduates working at jobs that do not require a degree, and only 27 percent working in jobs related to their degree programs, it's no wonder that public perception of higher education is increasingly negative. Tuition costs continue to outpace inflation, and, collectively, students are carrying more than $1.31 trillion in student loan debt that Americans expect to have repaid.

Let's review the statistics I cited in the introduction of this book, because they are very telling about the current American perception of higher education. Data compiled by Gallup reveal the following:

- ❤ Eighty percent of Americans agree or strongly agree that colleges and universities need to change to better meet the needs of today's students.
- ❤ Seventy-nine percent of Americans do not think that edu-

cation beyond high school is affordable for everyone in this country who needs it.

- Only 50 percent of university graduates believe that higher education is worth the cost.
- Only 6 percent of Americans with degrees strongly agree that college graduates in this country are well prepared for success in the workplace.

The data show that the American public understands what's at stake. Increasingly, students and families believe that higher education is a vehicle for meeting the needs of a global marketplace. Clearly, the staff and faculty at CSU-Global believe that as well, so it drives everything the university does and accomplishes.

IDENTIFYING OUR MARKET AND SERVING IT WELL

The success of CSU-Global rests firmly on knowing who our students are, what they need, and how to deliver what we promise.

CSU-Global has defined its market. It serves the non-traditional students who now comprise 75 percent of all college students. Nontraditional students don't have the luxury to be full-time students. They also work and care for their families, and they are leaders in their communities.

CSU-Global has determined the product its market needs. The university blends the best of what higher education offers with the knowledge of what a twenty-first-century workforce demands. It teaches its students critical-thinking skills, and then measures the extent to which they can demonstrate their knowledge. But the university also works closely with its faculty and with industry partners to prepare its students for in-demand jobs. CSU-Global teaches its students the skills they need to be "plug and play," the ability to step into a job and be successful on day one.

CSU-Global has decided how best to provide its products to its market. Nontraditional students need the flexibility that an online education provides. The university is not online to be an online university. It is online because it's a delivery mechanism for providing education to students who could not otherwise obtain a college degree.

If higher education intends to play a role in helping individuals and our nation succeed, these are the calculations every institution must make. Whom do you serve? What do they need? How can you best offer it to them? Differentiation and a clear mission are the keys to success.

CSU-Global is not a one-size-fits-all place, because this is no longer a one-size-fits-all economy. That's why listening to students, industry partners, and the marketplace matters. The world is increasingly interconnected, so CSU-Global is connected to all its stakeholders. The institution continually makes the adjustments needed to deliver on the promise it made: *to prepare nontraditional learners for workplace success in a global marketplace through education.*

IF WE CAN DO THIS, SO CAN YOU

CSU-Global hasn't cornered the market on what it takes to be successful in higher education. We've taken concepts and made them work for us, but they will work equally well elsewhere.

Every decision we make at CSU-Global is based on data, and data can be collected in every environment. Data can be shared across multiple departments and used to ensure that students are getting a return on their investment. Technology makes it possible to collect, share, and use data quickly and securely, whether online or in a brick-and-mortar institution.

Transparency, connectedness, and efficiency also are hallmarks of the CSU-Global success story. However, there is nothing about being an online university that gives us an edge in any of these areas.

Traditional colleges and universities can set tuition based on a budget that reflects what is truly required for student success, while driving down their operational and overhead expenses. Faculty and staff can work together to make students' lives easier, rather than sending them to the four corners of campus to get their needs met. Schools can lower administrative costs and hold each and every individual, from the maintenance staff to the president, accountable for their students' success.

A BRIGHT FUTURE

At CSU-Global, we expect our students to apply what they learn and to embrace the need for lifelong education, and we expect no less of ourselves as an institution. We will never stop learning and growing.

Higher education must evolve to be relevant in today's economy, so we will continue to look for ways in which CSU-Global can help frame this discussion. Currently, we are examining ways in which we can evaluate and promote new models of internships and apprenticeships, blending the best of what higher education and industry have to offer.

We are pursuing the best ways to prepare students for success in a world in which automation is replacing low-skilled labor and pushing people farther down the economic ladder. If these individuals don't possess the education and the critical-thinking skills to make decisions and function at a higher level inside of an organization, they will continue to fall behind, perpetuating a society of haves and have-nots.

Most important, through this book and related initiatives, we are sharing our story. CSU-Global is a small institution, but we are making our mark. We are financially stable without state and other funding. A full 98 percent of employers—a near perfect score—are satisfied or highly satisfied with the performance of CSU-Global graduates in their employ. And 94 percent of CSU-Global alumni agree that their program contributed to their workplace success.

CSU-Global may look and act differently from other institutions, but we are achieving unprecedented success as we continue to hold ourselves accountable to our students and to their workplace success. Our unending improvement toward that end is vital as we continue to contribute to the ongoing success of American competitiveness.

ABOUT THE AUTHOR

—

BECKY TAKEDA-TINKER, PHD, blends her passion for education with her experience in nonprofit governance and business leadership to lead Colorado State University–Global Campus. As president of CSU-Global, Takeda-Tinker champions data-driven, technology-based solutions to facilitate workplace success for adult learners. She started with CSU-Global as an instructor, and later, as dean, she worked to ensure the stability and success of the university. Takeda-Tinker has academic and workplace expertise in finance, leadership, and business management. With the mind of an entrepreneur and the soul of an educator, Takeda-Tinker is remaking higher education to advance American competitiveness.

Made in the USA
Coppell, TX
12 July 2020

30667796R00089